Collins

Edexcel GCSE 9-1
Business

Revision Guide

Stephanie Campbell, Helen Kellaway
and Tony Michaelides

About this Revision & Practice book

Revise

These pages provide a recap of everything you need to know for each topic.

You should read through all the information before taking the Quick Test at the end. This will test whether you can recall the key facts.

Quick Test

1. What does market segmentation mean?
2. Name **three** ways a market can be segmented.
3. How many features are used to produce a market map?
4. What can a market map identify for a business owner?

Practise

These topic-based questions appear shortly after the revision pages for each topic and will test whether you have understood the topic. If you get any of the questions wrong, make sure you read the correct answer carefully.

Review

These topic-based questions appear later in the book, allowing you to revisit the topic and test how well you have remembered the information. If you get any of the questions wrong, make sure you read the correct answer carefully.

Mix it Up

These pages feature a mix of questions for the different topics within a chapter. They will make sure you can recall the relevant information to answer a question without being told which topic it relates to.

Test Yourself on the Go

Visit our website at **collins.co.uk/collinsGCSErevision** and print off a set of flashcards. These pocket-sized cards feature questions and answers so that you can test yourself on all the key facts anytime and anywhere. You will also find lots more information about the advantages of spaced practice and how to plan for it.

Workbook

This section features even more topic-based questions as well as practice exam papers, providing further practice opportunities for each topic to guarantee the best results.

ebook

To access the ebook revision guide visit

collins.co.uk/ebooks

and follow the step-by-step instructions.

Contents

Contents

The Dynamic Nature of Business

You must be able to:

- Discuss the different reasons why new business ideas emerge
- Discuss how new business ideas emerge.

Starting a Business

- Businesses need to be dynamic to be successful and grow.
- A **dynamic business** sees meeting the changing needs of customers as important for its survival.
- Business ideas are generated because of:
  - changes in technology
  - changes in **consumers'** tastes
  - outdated goods and services.

Changes in Technology

- The popularity of the Internet and new technologies, Has led to new businesses being set up.
- Smart technology has generated new product ideas, from touchscreen phones to self-driving cars, and geo-location taxi services.
- Online marketplaces enable small businesses to set up and start selling online immediately.
- Consumers are now able to access a much larger marketplace by ordering goods and services from around the world via websites.
- Social media websites allow businesses to communicate closely with consumers and offer a platform for free promotion and advertising.

Changes in Consumers' Tastes

- Consumers' tastes can change over time.
- Businesses need to keep giving consumers what they want to keep the business current and to prevent consumers going to competitors.
- The popularity of the Internet means that consumers can easily research different businesses before making a choice to buy – this has led to an increase in price comparison websites.
- The increase in café culture has seen a rise in coffee chains and independent coffee shops on high streets.
- Changes in attitudes towards fast food, combined with income growth, has led to more consumers opting to dine in upmarket burger chains.

- Consumers have become more health conscious, giving rise to new gym chains, the need for personal trainers, and fitness-related goods and services.
- As consumers become more environmentally aware, they favour organic, free range products and products that use recyclable packaging.

Outdated Goods and Services

- As products become outdated, they are replaced with new business ideas that better meet the needs of consumers.
- USBs are being replaced with cloud storage, which prevents loss/damage to files.
- Portable CD players have been replaced with portable media players, allowing more music to be played from smaller devices.
- Consumers are opting to buy electric cars rather than petrol cars because they are less damaging to the environment.
- Petrol station car washes have been replaced by car washing enterprises located in convenient places for consumers, such as supermarket carparks.

Cloud Storage

How is a New Business Idea Generated?

- A new business idea will either be generated to fill a gap in the market or to improve an existing business idea.
- This means a business idea will either be a new original idea or be an adaptation of a good or service that is already on the market.
- A new business idea will be generated by an entrepreneur, e.g. drones.
- An entrepreneur may develop an existing business idea or will improve goods and services to better meet the needs of customers, e.g. supermarkets without manned checkouts.

The new version of the Mini (left) is an update of the older car (right).

Quick Test

1. How do dynamic businesses respond to consumer wants?
2. Name **three** reasons why new business ideas come about.
3. A business idea can be an original idea. What other way can a new business idea be generated?

Key Words

dynamic business
consumers
gap in the market
entrepreneur

Risk and Reward

You must be able to:

- Understand that entrepreneurs must establish potential risks and plan for them when starting up a new business
- Explain the potential rewards for starting up a new business.

Risk

- It is important for an entrepreneur to understand the things that can go wrong when setting up a new business; these are **risks**.
- Although there are a lot of risks associated with startups, risk occurs at every stage in business. The introduction of a new business idea is often seen as the riskiest stage of all.
- If an entrepreneur can address risks during the development stage of a new business idea, these risks can be reduced.
- Risks include: business failure, financial loss, lack of security.
- Business failure can be because of:
  - entrepreneurs not knowing their market well
  - not having enough money to start a business
  - poor decision making
  - competition or goods/services not meeting the needs of customers.

Business failure can happen to any size of business at any time.

- An entrepreneur can lose their own money they have put into the business and money borrowed from other sources.
- Many small businesses operate as sole traders and partnerships, as these have unlimited liability; these are the riskiest business startup options (see pages 38–39).
- Business owners can also lose personal possessions if the business runs up debts.

> **Key Point**
>
> Risks can include business failure, loss of money and lack of a secure income.

> **Key Point**
>
> Although risks can cause businesses to fail, with careful planning and research the risks can be reduced.

- Working for yourself means you do not have the security of a regular salary or wages. If a business is not successful, an entrepreneur can be at risk of not being able to pay bills such as rent or a mortgage.
- It is important for entrepreneurs to plan for potential risks and conduct relevant market research to understand how their product will/will not meet customer needs.

Reward

- The rewards for starting up a new business can include: business success, profit and personal independence.
- Some rewards are connected to money and are referred to as financial rewards, other rewards are non-financial, e.g. independence.
- Measuring the businesses sales, the amount of market share it holds or the profit made over time, are ways that can determine business success.
- Success can mean different things to different entrepreneurs, e.g. an online fashion blogger may consider subscribers or followers as a way of determining success, whereas a personal trainer will consider getting his/her clients to their desired weight/level of fitness as success.

- Profit is the difference between the revenue earned by a business and the costs of a business. Any profit that is gained goes to the business owners.
- An entrepreneur will make all the decisions for the business and can set what days they want to work. This independence is rewarding and encourages people to start their own businesses.

Key Point

Having a successful business, making a profit or being independent are potential rewards for starting up a business.

Key Point

Business revenue, costs and profit are covered on pages 28–29.

Quick Test

1. Name **three** risks a startup business may face.
2. How can entrepreneurs reduce the risk of business failure?
3. What non-financial rewards can a business startup provide?

Key Words

risks
market research
rewards
profit

The Role of Business Enterprise

You must be able to:

- Understand that the purpose of businesses is to produce goods and services that meet consumers' needs profitably
- Outline the different ways a business can add value to its products to increase worth
- Explain that the role of an entrepreneur is to organise the four factors of production to produce goods and services.

The Difference between Goods and Services

- A business will either provide goods or services to consumers.
- A good is a physical product that can be touched, e.g. a pair of trainers.
- Services are non-physical, e.g. a driving lesson.
- Product is a generic term used for both goods and services.

Key Point

Goods are physical products, such as a mobile phone. Services are non-physical, such as a bus journey.

Key Point

Consumer needs are covered on pages 14–15.

The Purpose of a Business

- Providing what consumers want is at the heart of a successful startup.
- A business owner needs to ensure their goods or services satisfy the needs of their consumers.
- If consumers' needs are not met, consumers will shop elsewhere.
- Consumers benefit from the choices available.

Adding Value

- An important purpose of a business is to add value to its goods/services.
- Adding value is the difference between the cost of the raw materials/components or of producing the good/service and the price that consumers are willing to pay for the good/service.
- Methods to add value include:
  - branding
  - quality
  - design
  - convenience
  - unique selling points (USPs).

Key Point

Methods of adding value include: branding, quality, convenience, design and unique selling points.

- **Branding** – this creates an image for a product that sets it apart from competitors and makes it easily recognisable by consumers; consumers will pay a higher price for a branded product than one that is unbranded, e.g. a designer fashion label.

- **Quality** – if a business provides a high-quality product, consumers will be prepared to pay a higher price, as they know it is premium, e.g. a restaurant that uses the best cuts of meat.
- **Design** – if a product has a unique feature or design, this makes it different from other products; consumers are willing to pay a higher price for something that has a special design or feature, e.g. a handmade product.
- **Convenience** – consumers are willing to pay more for a product if it saves them time, e.g. pre-chopped vegetables.
- **USPs** – this is a characteristic or feature of a product that makes the product unique, and that another business would find hard to copy, e.g. a special cake recipe.

- A successful business will likely use more than one method to add value.
- If a business can add value and keep costs low, the amount of profit will be increased.

> **Key Point**
>
> The four factors of production are: capital, land, labour and enterprise.

The Role of an Entrepreneur

- An entrepreneur needs four things to provide goods and services: capital, land, labour and enterprise.
- These are known as the four factors of production.
  - **capital** – man-made resources (goods used to produce other goods).
  - **land** – all natural resources, e.g. wheat or solar power.
  - **labour** – human input, e.g. skills or qualifications.
  - enterprise – skills and characteristics to manage the other three factors (capital, land, labour) and take risks.

- It is an entrepreneur's responsibility to organise the four factors of production to make goods and services that consumers want to buy.
- Organising these factors is risky and an entrepreneur must take careful consideration before making decisions.

> **Key Words**
>
> goods
> services
> product
> add value
> unique selling points
> factors of production
> enterprise

> **Quick Test**
>
> 1. What is the name of a physical product that can be touched?
> 2. Why do businesses exist?
> 3. What are the four factors of production that an entrepreneur must organise?

1 Explain why a business needs to be dynamic. [3]

To grow and expand successfuly,it needs to be dynamic

2 How can a business benefit from taking advantage of a gap in the market? [2]

A gap in the market is an advantage as it lets the business fit the customer needs more.

3 Which **one** of the following is not an example of why new business ideas come about? Tick the correct box. [1]

A Changes in technology ☑

B Changes in what consumers want ☐

C Businesses are not innovative ☐

D Product/services becoming obsolete ☐

4 How do changing consumer preferences impact businesses? [2]

5 What does the term 'risk' mean? [1]

Risk means taking a chance without knowing the outcome.

6 Explain why independence is a reward for starting up a business. [3]

Independence is a reward as the owner can now make all the choses for the business and for themselfs, like they can choose the hours they work

7 Explain how a lack of security is seen as a risk for an entrepreneur. [3]

Lack of security can lead to a risk for the owner as they may not get paid so they can't pay the bills or food leading them into debt.

8 Which **one** of the following would not lead to business failure?
Tick the correct box. [3]

A Not meeting the needs of customers ☐

B Poor decision making ☐

C Having a business plan ☑

D Not having the finance to cover all startup costs ☐

9 What is the purpose of a business? [1]

To provide goods and surives that satisfy the customer.

10 Explain why enterprise is an important factor of production. [3]

Enterprise is important as workers need skills to manage capital, land and labor but also be able to take risks.

11 What are the **five** ways in which a business can add value to its goods or services? [5]

Qualit, atst looks, function, brand, usp

12 Explain how branding adds value to a business's products. [3]

Branding adds value as it creates an image and puts an advantage against other brands.

Customer Needs

You must be able to:

- State different customer needs
- Explain the importance of businesses adapting to accommodate customer needs
- Evaluate possible rewards for businesses that meet their customers' needs.

What are Customer Needs?

- **Customer needs** are the specific wants or needs buyers have when purchasing a product.
- Customer needs include:
  - price
  - quality
  - choice
  - convenience
  - service.
- Businesses must understand what a customer wants when they buy their products.

How do Businesses Meet Customer Needs?

- Different customers don't all want the same things from a business. Think about it, do you watch the same films as your grandparents?
- Businesses produce goods and services that will satisfy the different wants of customers, e.g. Netflix has a variety of films available. Subscribers can choose between different age ranges to suit them, and different movie styles, depending on what they want to watch.
- Due to changes in fashion and taste, customers' needs are likely to change over time.

> **Key Point**
>
> Businesses keep in touch with their customers through market research (see pages 16–17).

- Successful businesses anticipate their customers' needs in advance to ensure they can stay ahead of competition and meet customer needs constantly.
- Businesses need to stay close to their customers to keep up to date with their needs.

Why is it Important for Businesses to Adapt to Meet Customer Needs?

- It's important for businesses to adapt so that:
  - they can target lots of different customers.
  - the same product can satisfy different customer needs.
  - a business does not lose customers to competitors.
  - the business can stay current and on trend.

How are Price and Quality Linked?

- Customers will try and get the best quality for the most reasonable price, e.g. a customer is willing to pay more for a burger from Gourmet Burger Kitchen than from McDonalds because they know that Gourmet Burger Kitchen is a more upmarket burger chain that uses better ingredients.
- Businesses need to ensure they price their goods or services at the right level, according to their perceived quality.

Why Meeting Customer Needs is Important

- Businesses can only survive if they have customers – so they have to focus on what they want.
- A business must have enough customers willing to pay a high enough price to cover costs and make a profit.
- Satisfied customers lead to more sales and revenue for a business.
- Other rewards of satisfied customers include: profit, good customer reviews, word of mouth, repeat purchases, and loyal customers.

> ### Key Point
>
> Businesses need to achieve the right balance to meet customer needs, e.g. having a good choice of products that are priced too high, will not meet the needs of customers who want low prices.

Quick Test

1. Name **three** different customer needs.
2. Why must businesses provide choice to customers?
3. Why would a customer pay more for a flight on British Airways than they would for an easyJet flight?
4. Explain why meeting customer needs is so important to a business.

Key Words

customer needs
customer reviews
repeat purchases

Market Research

You must be able to:

- Define and explain the purpose of market research
- Give examples of how businesses collect market research data
- Discuss how a business uses data collected from market research.

What is Market Research?

- **Market research** is the process of collecting information about what consumers want, **market trends** and competitors.
- For a small startup business, market research will be focused on finding out if there is enough demand to make the business idea successful.
- Market research helps entrepreneurs identify and understand customer needs.
- It can be used to:
  - identify a **gap in the market**
  - inform business decisions
  - reduce the risk of starting a business.

Primary Research

Primary research is collecting new information that meets the specific needs of a business.

- The information will not have been collected before.
- Examples include survey, questionnaire, focus group, observation.

Advantages
• Can ask questions that they need answers to
• The information is current
• The information won't have been seen by competitors

Disadvantages
• Can be expensive
• Can be time-consuming
• The results may be inaccurate

Secondary Research

Secondary research involves using data that already exists, or data that has already been gathered by someone else.

- Examples include Internet, market reports, government reports.

Advantages
• The data is easy to find
• Cheap or free to obtain
• Can give a good overview of the market

Disadvantages
• It may have been collected for a different purpose and so may be inaccurate
• Can be out of date
• May not be specific to the business needs

> ### Key Point
>
> Business decisions should be based on information collected from market research.

> ### Key Point
>
> Small startup businesses are not likely to have a large sum of money for market research. This will limit the methods they can use.

Social Media and Market Research Data

- Social media can be used by entrepreneurs to collect research via feedback from comments, reviews, surveys or online focus groups about their business or to find out how customers feel about competitors.
- Current trends can be tracked using hashtags and by following popular posts.
- The greater the activity on social media, the more likely it is that a business will receive responses to market research.
- Collecting data can be quick and cheap.
- The data can be collected in real time so is up to date.
- Businesses can respond to their customers immediately.
- The data collected can be used to inform business decisions.

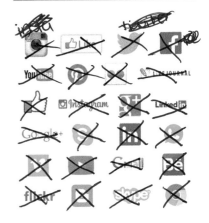

Qualitative Data and Quantitative Data

- Quantitative data is numerical and can be measured easily.
- Closed questions from a questionnaire can be put into a graph or chart.
- Qualitative data is opinions, judgements and feelings and so cannot be put into a numerical form.
- Qualitative data can be collected during focus groups, in which open-ended questions are asked to gain in-depth answers.
- Quantitative and qualitative data should be used together to inform decision making.
- Qualitative and quantitative data can be derived from both primary and secondary market research.

Considering Data Before Use

- A business must determine how reliable research is before making decisions based upon it.
- Market research can be misleading if the right information is not collected from the right people.
- Market research may be unreliable as market research questions can be worded in a way that lead people to a certain answer; respondents may not give true answers, and the sample of people used for the research may not be large enough to determine how the entire market feels.
- Some businesses have been successful without conducting any market research.

Quick Test

1. Define market research.
2. What are the **two** types of market research?
3. What is the name given to data that can be interpreted in a numerical way?

Market Segmentation

You must be able to:

- Explain how businesses identify and use market segmentation to target customers
- Discuss how market mapping can identify gaps in the market and the competition.

What is Market Segmentation?

- **Market segmentation** involves breaking down a market into smaller groups, called segments.
- Each of the different groups will contain people that have similar characteristics and have similar wants and needs.
- Information from market research will usually determine which market segment to target goods or services at.
- A business can then focus on how best to sell to that **target market** and meet the customer needs of that group.

How are Markets Segmented?

By Location
- Grouping customers based on where they live.
- A business may decide to focus on selling to customers in a small local area, e.g. a café, or in a busy town.

By Demographics
- **Demographics** group customers based on statistical data relating to the population, e.g. resident status – home owner or renter.
- A business may consider whether they are targeting families or couples for their product.

By Lifestyle
- Grouping customers on how they live their lives and the choices they make.
- With healthy living and fitness a growing trend, a business selling pure fruit smoothies will target health-conscious customers.

By Income
- Grouping customers based on how much they earn, the job that they do or their social class.
- If a business has a luxury good or service, they will target customers with high earnings.

By Age
- Grouping customers according to their age.
- A youth club owner will want to target teenagers.

Key Point

Markets can be segmented by location, demographics, lifestyle, income and age.

Market Mapping

- When a business has decided on a market segment to target, they will need to decide what is important to that market and where to place their product within this market.
- A diagram can be used to position and compare products in a market; this diagram is called a market map.
- Market mapping is used by businesses to identify where a product will be placed in a market compared to other similar products in the same market.
- A diagram is drawn up with two axes and each axis represents a feature of the market. These features are based on the needs of the target market.
  These features can be:
  - high price – low price
  - high quality – low quality
  - large range of services – small range of services
  - very colourful – no colour.
- Goods or services from different businesses are placed on the map according to how they meet the features.
- Products can be differentiated based on the features to make a business's product stand out.
- A business can look for gaps in the market map to identify possible business opportunities.
- Competitors can be identified and businesses can look for ways to improve on what they are offering.
- A business must take caution when identifying gaps in the market. The gap may be due to there being no market available. For example, customers will not buy a product that has a high price but is of low quality.

A market map

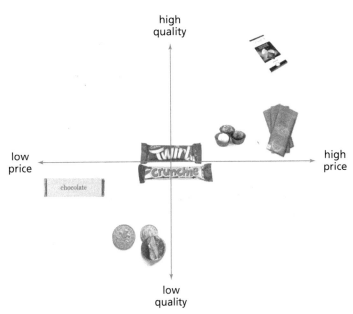

Key Point

Market mapping is key to finding out gaps in the market and the identity of competitions.

Quick Test

1. What does market segmentation mean?
2. Name three ways a market can be segmented.
3. How many features are used to produce a market map?
4. What can a market map identify for a business owner?

Key Words

market segmentation
target market
demographics
market map

The Competitive Environment

You must be able to:

- Understand that businesses operate in a competitive environment
- Discuss the strengths and weaknesses of competitors
- Discuss the impact of competition on business decision making.

Competitive Environment

- Small startup businesses must be aware of and investigate other businesses offering similar goods/services.
- Competition occurs when separate businesses provide goods and services to the same group of customers.
- A **competitive environment** is a market where there are many businesses selling similar goods and services, e.g. consider the choice available when buying a smartphone – this is a competitive environment.
- Businesses operating in competitive environments need to find ways to make their goods and services different from the competition; this is referred to as **differentiation**.
- To investigate the strengths and weaknesses of potential competition, a business will look at different criteria.

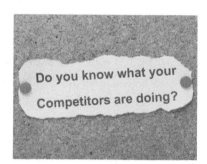

Do you know what your Competitors are doing?

How do Businesses Compete?

Price

- One business may offer lower prices to attract consumers.
- Price lowering can result in more sales but will also increase costs for the business, as they must produce more to meet the increased demand – if they don't make enough extra sales, their overall revenue may be less than before and thus profits may be lower.
- Reducing prices may also encourage other businesses to reduce prices as well, creating a price war. If prices are reduced too much, consumers associate the goods or services with poor quality.

Quality

- A business may decide to focus on quality and choose to offer better quality goods/services.
- A high-quality product can attract consumers that want a good quality product, and are also willing to pay a higher price.
- Using better quality raw materials or ingredients or offering additional customer support will increase costs for a business.

> **Key Point**
>
> Businesses need to consider the strengths and weaknesses of competitors based on: price, quality, location, product range and customer service.

Location

- A business may have a superior location over another business – it may be easy to access and be more convenient for consumers – resulting in higher sales.
- A factory may have good transport links for suppliers and distribution.
- An online business may have a more user-friendly website.
- A business may not be able to change location but can instead focus on offering more to customers, e.g. free wi-fi or comfortable seating.

Product Range

- Having a large product range gives consumers more choice and businesses can meet different customer needs.
- A business may decide to specialise in a specific good or service and this will attract consumers that want a more dedicated service.

Customer Service

- A business can decide to compete through offering a good selling experience or excellent after-sales service.
- Good customer service can help to secure repeat custom.
- Satisfied consumers leave good reviews and provide word-of-mouth recommendations.
- Training staff in good customer service can increase training costs.

Competition and Decision Making

- Operating in a competitive environment is more challenging for a small startup business. Rather than trying to match the strengths of competitors, a small business will need to focus on differentiating their goods/services.
- Market research is key here to stay up-to-date with the actions of competitors.
- Once a business can identify potential opportunities to better meet customer needs, they can improve what they have on offer.
- A business can gain a competitive advantage by:
  - buying cheaper raw materials to make cost savings
  - offering exceptional customer service
  - providing excellent quality
  - offering promotions and loyalty discounts.

Quick Test

1. Define a competitive environment.
2. Name **one** disadvantage of competing on price.
3. How does competition affect a business's decision making?

Key Words

competitive environment
differentiation
product range
competitive advantage

1   Which **one** of the following is an example of a product becoming outdated?
    Tick the correct box.   [1]

    A   Portable CD players   ☑

    B   Smart phones   ☐

    C   Virtual reality headsets   ☐

    D   Cloud storage   ☐

2   How has the rise of web technologies and the use of smartphones benefitted businesses?   [3]

_____

_____

_____

3   What does the term 'dynamic business' mean?   [1]

_____

4   Explain how a business can adapt an existing business idea.   [3]

A business can adapt an existing business idea
by changing the look/athetic, quality or
function

5   What are the potential rewards for setting up a business?   [3]

Rewords can be finacial, like getting the
profit or non-finacial like getting to chose
the hours they work.

6   Why are sole traders and partnerships the riskiest startup options?   [2]

They are risky because they dont get any
help unlike with a franchies.

7 What factors can an entrepreneur use to measure their business success?   [3]

8 How can an entrepreneur avoid risks when starting up a new business?   [2]

They avoid risk by finding out pt reasearch to find what customers want or need

9 What is the difference between a good and a service?
   Use examples to explain your answer.   [2]

A good is something tangable and a survice is an exprence/something you cant tuch.

10 What does the term 'unique selling point' mean?   [1]

Charactertstic that makes a product diffrent or stand out.

11 Why is it important for a business to add value to its goods and services?   [3]

12 How can design help a business to add value?   [3]

1. What is meant by the term 'customer needs'? [1]

   It's the spesific needs or wants of a ~~bu~~ buyer

2. Why do customer needs differ? [1]

   Customer needs differ as prices, and place effect what the business.

3. Why is it important for a business to identify customer needs? [3]

   Identifing customer needs so they can stay ahead of businesses compotition so more sales can be achived to get more rivenu.

4. Name **three** ways a business can collect primary market research. [3]

   A business can conduct primary research by using ~~social meetia~~ surrays, focus groups, observation and questioncir.

5. Why are small startup businesses limited in the market research methods they can use? [2]

   Startup business is limited because they have a limited costs.

6. How can a business use social media to collect market research data? [3]

   Social media helps a business to collect data as it reaches a wide range of people and its also quick and cheap.

7. What is the difference between qualitative data and quantitative data? [2]

   Qualitative data is ~~etad~~ data is the oppineun of the person and quantative data is numrical and easy to measure.

8 Identify **four** market segments a business could use to target potential customers. [4]

age

gender location

income

lifestyle.

9 How are markets segmented by lifestyle? [2]

Life style as some may have diffrent belifes and ethics effecting their choses.

10 What information can a business gather by market mapping? [3]

By market mapping it help shows an area gap in the market and the commpertition.

11 What is the impact of competition on a business's decision making? [3]

12 Explain how a business can achieve success in a competitive environment. [1]

They can successed in competitive enviorment by deferentuating the product.

Business Aims and Objectives

You must be able to:

- Explain what business aims and objectives are when starting up
- Understand the difference between financial and non-financial aims and objectives
- Explain why aims and objectives differ between businesses.

What are Aims and Objectives?

- **Aims** are goals for a business; they explain what a business wants to achieve in the long term.
- **Objectives** are the short-term steps a business takes to achieve its aims.
- **SMART** objective setting is often used to make sure objectives are specific, measurable, achievable, realistic and timely.

Key Point
Aims and objectives can vary for different types of organisations and can be financial or non-financial.

Why Does a Business Set Aims and Objectives?

- To allow the business to share its direction with staff so they know what to focus on and are motivated to perform.
- To enable a business to measure its performance.
- To help a business plan for the future.

Financial Aims and Objectives for Different Types of Organisations

- Private sector businesses often have aims and objectives that maximise their profit, market share or expand the business.
- Private sector businesses are privately owned.
- Public sector businesses are more likely to focus on delivering a service to customers and keeping costs to a minimum.
- Public sector businesses are run by the government for the benefit of society, e.g. schools, hospitals, fire service.
- Not-for-profit organisations, or charities, aim to fundraise or collect donations for specific causes, e.g. The Royal Society for the Prevention of Cruelty to Animals (RSPCA).
- Social enterprises use business techniques to sell products or services for profit, which is invested to benefit society or the environment, rather than paid out to individual shareholders, e.g. Divine chocolate.

Financial Aims and Objectives

- Financial aims and objectives typically relate to money.
- When a business starts trading, often its aim is survival, which means to be able to simply operate (survive) by meeting its costs in the beginning stages, which tend to be high.
- Many businesses aim to maximise profit.
- Some businesses aim to increase the volume of sales of products or services.
- Other businesses have an aim to increase their market share, which is the percentage of sales held by a business in a particular market.
- Some entrepreneurs begin a business to provide them with financial security and personal wealth.

Non-financial Aims and Objectives

- Non-financial aims and objectives relate to goals which are not money-related.
- Having a business with social objectives, e.g. providing goods and services that are kind to the environment or aim to eliminate poverty, is important for many organisations.
- Personal satisfaction is key for many business people.
- Many entrepreneurs aim to challenge themselves with new ventures.
- Some entrepreneurs aim for independence so that they don't have to work for someone else.
- Having more control over their work/life balance might be an aim for some entrepreneurs.

Some charities, such as Oxfam, operate shops to raise money for the causes they support.

> **Key Point**
>
> A social enterprise is an organisation that raises **capital** for good causes by using traditional business techniques. All profits are reinvested back into the cause, rather than shared out to shareholders.

> **Key Words**
>
> aims
> objectives
> SMART
> profit
> survival
> sales
> capital
> market share
> financial security
> social objectives
> personal satisfaction

> **Quick Test**
>
> 1. Explain the difference between an 'aim' and an 'objective'.
> 2. Explain why a business should set aims and objectives.
> 3. Explain the difference between 'financial' and 'non-financial' aims and objectives, giving an example for each type.

Business Revenues, Costs and Profit

You must be able to:

- Understand the concept and know how to calculate different business formulae relating to revenues, costs and profit
- Calculate total interest as a percentage of total repayment for a mortgage or loan
- Identify break-even levels of output and margins of safety on break-even diagrams and interpret impacts of change in revenues and costs.

All formulae can be found on page **139**.

Revenues, Costs and Profit

Most businesses will face **one-off costs** when they first begin to pay for machinery and property, and will make an initial **loss** because it takes time to attract paying customers.

	Revenue	Direct costs	Indirect costs	Fixed costs	Variable costs	Total costs	Profit (loss)
Definition	Cash inflows	Cash outflows directly related to the production of goods and services	Cash outflows not directly related to the production of goods and services	Cash outflows that stay the same regardless of the level of output	Cash outflows that vary with levels of output	All costs added together are total costs	The amount of revenue left after deduction of costs; a positive figure is profit, a negative figure is a loss
Formula	selling price × units sold	n/a	n/a	total costs – variable costs	variable cost per unit × number of units sold	fixed costs + variable costs	revenue – total costs
Example/s	Revenue for the sale of goods or services	Labour, packaging, ingredients	Insurance, heating, director's salary	Salaries, rent, advertising	Wages, raw materials, packaging	n/a	n/a

Interest

- Sometimes a business needs to raise finance by borrowing money.
- This borrowing can come from friends or family who are willing to help, or from a bank.
- The business will probably have to pay an **interest rate** on the money borrowed.
- Interest rates charged are expressed as a percentage per annum (p.a.), e.g. 2% p.a, so, for example, if a business borrows £10 000 from a bank for one year at 2% p.a., it will need to repay the bank £10 200 at the end of the year.
- A business may make enough profit to put some cash into a savings account with a bank which pays interest – this is often a way for a business to earn extra revenue as the interest it receives on its savings provides more income.
- Interest is covered in more detail on pages 32–33.

Contribution, Break Even and Margin of Safety

A business can use formulas for contribution per unit, break even and margin of safety to determine the impact of selling prices and costs of making and selling products.

	Contribution per unit	Break even	Margin of safety
Definition	How much each sale contributes towards fixed costs; any further sales are a contribution towards profit	Where total costs = total revenue; at this point, a business is not making any loss or any profit	The amount of products made and sold beyond the break-even point up to the actual level of output
Formula	selling price – variable costs per unit	fixed costs / contribution per unit	level of output – break-even point

Worked Example

- – Cookies selling price £1
- – Fixed costs of £10 000 per month
- – Variable costs of 20p per cookie
- – 15 000 cookies are made and sold each month

- • Therefore:
  - – Contribution is £1 – 20p = 80p per cookie
  - – Break even is £10 000 / 80p = 12 500 cookies
  - – Margin of safety is 15 000 – 12 500 cookies = 3500 cookies

Key Point

Beware, break even relies on products being made and sold. If a business makes no sales, it will not break even.

Break Even

- • Using a break-even chart (or diagram) is a visual way of showing where total revenue meets total costs; the break-even point is where the total revenue line crosses the total costs line.
- • Break even is a useful tool for a business to calculate how many products or services it needs to make and sell at a certain selling price in order to cover all its costs.
- • Any change in selling price or total costs will have an affect on the break-even point, e.g. if the selling price increases, fewer products will need to be sold.

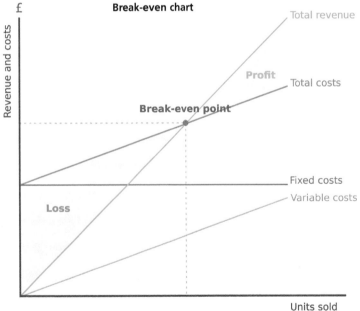

Break-even chart

Quick Test

1. Define 'fixed costs' and explain how they are different to 'variable costs'.
2. What is meant by 'contribution per unit'?
3. Explain how you could calculate break even using the contribution formula.

Key Words

one-off costs
loss
level of output
total costs
revenue
variable costs
fixed costs
interest rate
contribution per unit
break even
margin of safety

Cash and Cash-flow

You must be able to:

- Explain the importance of cash to a business
- Understand the difference between cash and profit
- Calculate and interpret cash-flow forecasts.

What is Cash-flow?

- **Cash-flow** is the flow of cash in and out of a business.
- **Cash inflow** is cash paid into a business from a variety of sources, e.g. sales, payments from customers, bank interest, sale of assets, bank loan capital.
- **Cash outflow** is cash paid out of a business, e.g. suppliers, wages, loan repayments, overheads, advertising costs.
- A cash surplus (also known as positive net cash-flow) is when a business experiences more cash inflows than cash outflows over the same period.
- A cash deficit is when a business experiences more cash outflows than cash inflows over the same period (also known as a negative cash-flow).

> **Key Point**
>
> Net cash-flow is the difference between cash inflows and cash outflows.

Why is Cash-flow so Important?

- Cash is critical to the survival of a business.
- Having too little cash when bills are due is known as **insolvency**, which means the business will fail if it cannot pay its bills on time.
- Having too much cash means the business is not earning any return, so it would be better to invest the money in new machinery to increase production or put it into a savings account that pays interest.

> **Key Point**
>
> If a business is unable to pay its bills, it risks becoming insolvent, which means being unable to pay debts when they are due.

The Difference Between Cash and Profit

- **Cash** is about timing – it is simply a record of when a business's cash inflows and cash outflows are due.
- **Profit** is: total revenue – total costs and is calculated immediately after a sale.
- A business may be highly profitable but if it does not have sufficient cash to pay its bills when they are due it risks becoming insolvent, leading to business failure.

> **Key Point**
>
> Profit and cash aren't the same thing. Profit is recorded immediately after a sale, whereas cash is recorded as and when it is received into or spent by a business.

What is a Cash-flow Forecast?

- Cash inflows and outflows are rarely the same amount each month so cash levels in a business fluctuate.
- Cash-flow forecasts show future cash inflows and outflows and are normally shown on a weekly or monthly basis.
- The opening balance for each month is the same amount as the closing balance from the previous month.

How a cash-flow forecast can help a business	
Predicts when cash flows in and out of a business	Financially plan ahead to minimise unexpected cash fluctuations
Highlights future cash surpluses and deficits	Make comparisons with previous periods to identity cash improvements or deterioration
Can be referred back to after cash transactions have been made to check they were correctly forecast	Be more financially accurate, which can help with overall business planning

What can Affect a Cash-flow Forecast?
- Sales might not be consistent.
- Customers might be unable to pay, meaning cash inflows will be less than forecast.
- Costs may change or unexpected costs may occur.
- Ordering too much stock.

Ways to Improve Cash-flow

A business can improve cash-flow by:
- Encouraging customers to pay up front.
- Sending prompt invoices.
- Chasing late payments from customers.
- Selling debts to a factoring company.
- Selling assets.
- Negotiating supplier trade credit terms.
- Using just in time stock ordering methods (see page 92).
- Arranging an overdraft facility to allow for negative balances.

Quick Test

1. Explain what is meant by the term 'cash-flow forecast'.
2. Explain why cash is so important to a business.
3. What is the difference between cash and profit?
4. Suggest **three** ways in which a business can improve its cash-flow.

Key Words

cash-flow
cash inflow
cash outflow
insolvency
cash-flow forecast
opening balance
closing balance

Sources of Business Finance

You must be able to:

- Identify sources of finance for business startups and for established businesses
- Explain short-term sources of finance available
- Explain long-term sources of finance available.

What are Sources of Finance?

- Sources of finance are *where* a business can obtain money from.
- Sources of finances assist with business start up.
- Sources of finances assist with operating costs, e.g. salaries, supplies, electricity bills.
- Sources of finance help with the expansion costs of a business, e.g. investing in new technologies.

Key Point

Overdrafts tend to be on a variable rate of interest, which means if the Bank of England decides to raise the bank base rate, businesses have to pay more interest on any borrowing they have on overdrafts.

Short-term Finance

- Short-term sources of finance are for small amounts of borrowing, which must be repaid within one year.
- There are different types of short-term finance:

Short-term finance option	Explained	Advantages	Disadvantages
Overdraft facility	An overdraft is when a bank allows a business to withdraw more money than it has in its account and pay it back later.	Quick, convenient, flexible; interest paid only on the amount of money borrowed and for the amount of time it is borrowed.	High, variable rates of interest; a bank may not grant the facility and can remove it at any time.
Trade credit	Trade credit is when a business receives goods from a supplier immediately but agrees to pay for them later.	A business receives payment from customers before paying suppliers, removing the need to raise its own finance.	Not all suppliers offer trade credit; suppliers might charge a higher selling price. New businesses may not be offered trade credit until financial trust is gained.

Long-term Finance

- Long-term sources of finance tend to be for larger amounts of money that are needed for longer periods of time, e.g. for startup purposes or for business expansion. There are different types of long-term finance – see opposite page for details.

Long-term finance option	Explained	Advantages	Disadvantages
Personal savings	Personal savings are the owner's own money.	Quick and easy to obtain; no interest.	Might need the money for personal reasons. Might not want to risk losing the money.
Retained profits	Retained profit is profit made and kept from previous trading years.	Quick and easy to obtain; no interest.	Might need the money for other needs; might not have any retained profit (especially if a new business).
Venture capital	Experienced business people with large capital offer venture capital to invest.	Large capital sums; no need to repay; no interest; risk carried by venture capitalists; business advice and experience offered.	Loss of control of decisions; profit is shared; may cause conflict with existing shareholders.
Share capital	Share capital is when a business owner sells shares in the business.	No need to repay; no interest. Private limited companies can retain as much control as possible by inviting family and friends to buy shares. Public limited companies can benefit from this quick way to raise significant capital.	Profit is shared; may cause conflict with existing shareholders; loss of control; financial information becomes public. For private limited companies, finding investors might be difficult; for public limited companies, greater public scrutiny of business performance. For public limited companies, there is loss of control in the business and financial data becomes public.
Bank loan	A loan is a sum of money lent by a bank to a business to repay in monthly repayments.	Business retains control over business; does not have to share profits; fixed loan repayments, so if interest rates increase, loan repayments will remain the same.	Takes time to arrange; interest is charged; bank might not grant loan; inflexible as repayments must be made on time. Collateral is often required (which is something valuable pledged by the business as security if the business fails to make its repayments).
Crowdfunding	An online appeal made to attract multiple investors who wish to put in small amounts each – this is crowdfunding.	Risk is shared amongst many; no interest; can reach a wide number of investors; acts as a method of promotion; a good way of testing a business idea; does not need to be repaid.	If the overall target funds are not reached, finance is returned to investors; the reputation of the business may suffer if fundraising fails; a business idea may be copied by anyone who sees it on the Internet; profits are shared.
Sale of assets	When a business sells an item of value, it is a sale of assets.	No interest; easy and convenient; creates valuable space.	Assets may not realise full market price or not sell at all; can be seen as a desperate measure; may regret selling assets that are needed in the future.

Quick Test

1. Explain the difference between short-term and long-term finance.
2. Explain the benefits of trade credit for a business.
3. Discuss the differences between an overdraft facility and a loan.

Key Words

short-term sources of finance
overdraft
trade credit
long-term sources of finance
personal savings
retained profit
venture capital
share capital
loan
crowdfunding
sale of assets

1 What are the **five** different customer needs? [5]

_____

_____

_____

_____

_____

2 Why is it important for businesses to anticipate customer needs? [2]

_____

_____

_____

3 How do customers link quality and price? [1]

_____

4 Name **three** benefits to a business of providing goods and services that customers want. [3]

_____

_____

_____

5 What is the main focus of market research for small startup businesses? [1]

_____

_____

6 What is the difference between primary and secondary market research? [2]

_____

_____

7 Give **two** examples of how a business can collect qualitative data. [2]

_____

_____

8 What is meant by market segmentation? [2]

_____

_____

9 Why does a business use market mapping? [2]

_____

_____

_____

10 Explain the problem with market mapping. [1]

_____

_____

11 Why is it important for a business to consider the strengths and weaknesses of competitors? [1]

_____

_____

12 Name **one** way a business can gain a competitive advantage. [1]

_____

1. Why would an organisation set aims and objectives? [2]

2. Give examples of **two** businesses whose objectives are likely to differ. Explain why they are different. [3]

3. State **three** financial aims and objectives of a business. [3]

4. What is a variable cost? [2]

5. What is the formula for Total Costs? [1]

6. A business has a selling price for their product of £10 and their variable cost per unit is £6. Calculate the contribution per unit. [1]

7. What does the term 'break even' mean? [2]

8　From the following break-even chart identify the break-even point and
　the margin of safety.　　　　　　　　　　　　　　　　　　　　　　　　[2]

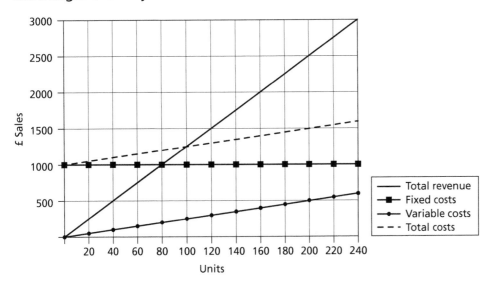

....

....

9　Give **two** examples of a cash outflow.　　　　　　　　　　　　　　　　[2]

....

....

10　What is the formula for Total Profit?　　　　　　　　　　　　　　　　　[1]

....

11　Explain what venture capital is.　　　　　　　　　　　　　　　　　　　[3]

....

....

....

12　Explain how selling assets could help the cash-flow of a business.　　　[3]

....

....

....

The Options for Startups and Small Businesses

You must be able to:

- Discuss the concept of limited liability
- Explain the advantages and disadvantages of different types of business ownership
- Discuss the option of starting up and running a franchise operation.

Liability

- **Liability** is the legal responsibility that a business owner has to pay his/her business's debts.
- The two types of liability are limited liability and unlimited liability.
- Different startups have different liability.

Limited Liability

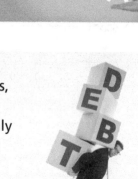

- There is a legal difference between the business owner and the business, meaning that owners have limited liability.
- If the business incurs debts, they belong to the business. Owners will only lose the money they have invested in the business.
- A **private limited company (Ltd)** has limited liability.

Unlimited Liability

- There is no legal difference between the owner and the business – the business owner is the business.
- The owner is legally responsible for the actions of the business and the business's debts – this is unlimited liability.
- If the business has debts, the owner may need to sell their personal belongings to pay the debts.
- **Business ownership** types that have unlimited liability: **sole trader** and **partnerships**.

Sole Trader

- The business is owned by one owner who has full control, although people can be employed as workers.
- The owner has unlimited liability.
- Examples: tutor, photographer, website designer.

Advantages	Disadvantages
<ul><li>Easy to set up – no fees</li><li>Owner keeps all profits</li><li>The owner is their own boss (self-employed)</li><li>Financial information about the company doesn't have to be made public</li></ul>	<ul><li>Personal belongings are at risk (unlimited liability)</li><li>Difficult to raise money</li><li>Earnings are lost if the owner is sick or takes a holiday</li></ul>

Partnership

- A partnership is a business owned by two or more partners.
- Partners share control and decision making.

- Unlimited liability for all partners unless the partners set up a Limited Liability Partnership (LLP) where partners will only be liable for what they have invested.
- Examples: doctors, dentists, vets, solicitors.

Advantages	Disadvantages
• More capital can be raised by partners • Partners can bring a range of skills • Financial information about the business doesn't have to be made public • Problems and decisions are shared	• Unlimited liability (unless a Limited Liability Partnership) • Partners may have disagreements • Profits are shared • If a partner dies or becomes bankrupt, the partnership will have to close

Private Limited Company

- Created by people who know each other.
- The owners are called shareholders. There must be at least one shareholder.
- Owners must register the business as a company (incorporation) with Companies House and have 'Ltd' after the company name.
- The shareholders each have limited liability.
- Examples of private limited companies: Moonpig.com, Cath Kidston, Eddie Stobart.

 **Key Point**

Unlimited liability means owners can lose personal possessions if their business has debts. Limited liability reduces the risk faced by owners as debts will belong to the business, not the owner.

Advantages	Disadvantages
• Limited liability • Shares can be sold to friends and family to raise money • Managers can be employed to run the business	• It is a legal requirement to file the company's accounts and this information is public • More administration involved to get started as a private limited company • Shares cannot be sold to the public

Franchising

- A franchise is an arrangement between an established business (the franchisor) that allows other businesses or individuals (franchisee/s) the right to sell goods and services using its name, trademark and business processes.
- A franchisee buys into an established business (franchise) but operates it as an independent business, e.g. Costa, Subway.

Advantages to the franchisee	Disadvantages to the franchisee
• The brand and customer base is already established • A high chance the business will be successful • Support and training is provided by the franchisor, e.g. marketing and staff training	• Startup fees can be expensive • Franchisor has to be paid a percentage of the revenue • Little control and flexibility – products are already created and decisions made • Complicated application process

> **Quick Test**

1. Which startup options have unlimited liability?
2. Name three disadvantages of being a sole trader.
3. What is franchising?

> **Key Words**

liability	partnership
limited liability	shareholders
unlimited liability	incorporation
private limited company (Ltd)	Companies House
business ownership	franchise
sole trader	franchisor
	franchisee

Business Location

You must be able to:

- Discuss the factors that influence business location
- Explain how the Internet has made an impact on location decisions for businesses.

Choosing a Business Location

- **Business location** is the place where a business operates.
- For some businesses location is very important, e.g. a barber shop needs to be in a convenient location for customers.
- Some small businesses do not need a physical location and can set up and run online.

The right location for a business will depend on:
- nature of the business
- market
- labour
- materials
- competitors.

Business Location and the Nature of the Business

- Some business owners start operating from home or operate solely online.
- Businesses in the primary sector (providing raw materials) need to be where the raw materials are located, e.g. a fisherman has to be near the sea.
- Businesses in the secondary sector (manufacturing, processing, assembly) need to be located in areas where transport links are good so that supplies can be brought in with ease and finished products can be sent out to be sold.
- Businesses in the secondary sector must be near skilled labour.
- Businesses in the secondary sector might start small and then rent a factory close to where the product is sold.
- Businesses in the tertiary sector (service-based) should be located close to or with easy access to their customers, e.g. a hotel should be close to tourist attractions or transport links.

Market

- Customers need to have easy access to goods and services in order to buy them.
- Locating close to other businesses can be important, e.g. coffee shops are often located on high streets so that tired shoppers can stop for a rest.

Labour

- A business needs to be near suitably skilled staff who are willing to work for the wages offered by the business.

Materials

- It is important for a business that uses raw materials that are bulky or heavy to be located close to the source of these raw materials.
- This will lower the production costs for the business.

Competitors

- Customers want choice, so a startup business may decide to locate near competitors because that is where the customers are, allowing the business to be another option should the customer decide to shop around.

The Impact of the Internet

- The Internet has now made it easier for some businesses to get started without the need for business premises.
- Businesses can sell goods easily through sites such as Etsy and ebay.
- Businesses can offer services through agency sites such as PeoplePerHour or Rated People.
- The Internet has led to growth in outsourcing, which has led to manufacturing companies moving their production to cheap overseas locations.
- The marketplace (where buyers and sellers meet) can be online so a business does not need to be located close to customers.

The Marketing Mix

You must be able to:

- Define the marketing mix and understand the importance of each element
- Explain the importance of a balanced marketing mix to operate in a competitive environment
- Explain how changing consumer needs impact the marketing mix
- Discuss the impact of technology on the marketing mix.

Elements of the Marketing Mix

- The **marketing mix** is a combination of four factors a business must consider to meet customer needs, known as the 4Ps: price, product, promotion and place.
- The 4Ps complement each other and a business needs to get the right balance (mix) of them, e.g. high-quality materials used to make a product will lead to a high selling price.
- The marketing mix is different for each business and changes over time.

Price

- The price that a business charges for their goods or services should allow a profit to be made.
- If a product is a high price, the quality is usually high.
- A low price may be used by a startup business to attract customers.

Product

- The product must meet customer needs.
- A business must consider its product range, brand and unique selling point/s.

Promotion

- Promotion creates awareness, boosts sales, builds a brand and communicates the features of a product.
- Promotion can be in the form of advertising, e.g. online, local newspapers or radio (for small businesses), or by using public relations and special offers.

Place

- Place is about how the product reaches customers – where and when they want it.
- A business can sell directly, through the Internet or from a business premise.
- Another selling option is through retailers or wholesalers.

Balancing the Marketing Mix

- The competitive environment of a business determines which element of the marketing mix is most important.

> **Key Point**
>
> The marketing mix is the combination of price, product, promotion and place.

- Price is important for a business located on a busy high street, but less important for an online web developer that focuses on making a creative and functional product for their client.
- A business may choose to opt for a low price to persuade customers to try their product; this may create a price war as other businesses reduce their prices.
- Small businesses can't reduce prices too much because they have higher costs to begin with.
- Modifying each element in the marketing mix establishes a differentiated product, enabling a business to be competitive.

Changing Customer Needs and the Marketing Mix

- A business has to conduct research to stay up-to-date with the needs of customers and make adjustments to the marketing mix.
- When a new product is introduced the marketing mix will be different to when the product is established and the brand has grown.

Technology and the Marketing Mix

- Changes in technology, e.g. e-commerce and digital communication, affect the marketing mix.

- **Place** – a small business can build a large customer base through selling online – they can target customers anywhere in the world and don't need to have a physical business premises.
- **Promotion** – digital communication, available through websites, email and social media gives businesses new promotion opportunities. A web-banner can be placed on multiple websites at a fraction of the cost of a billboard poster.
- **Price** – customers have more access to information, this makes them more knowledgeable about prices through comparison websites, so some businesses may have to change their prices to remain competitive. A business may be able to lower prices due to cost savings made from using technology in the production process.
- **Product** – social media and online customer reviews allow businesses to conduct market research and get first-hand comments from customers to identify how to meet their needs.

> **Quick Test**
>
> 1. Which element of the marketing mix involves communicating the features of a product?
> 2. How will operating in a competitive environment impact a business's marketing mix?
> 3. How has technology made an impact on the price element of the marketing mix?

> **Key Words**
>
> marketing mix
> public relations
> retailer
> wholesaler
> e-commerce
> digital communication

Business Plans

You must be able to:

- State the elements a business plan contains
- Explain the role and importance of a business plan.

What is a Business Plan?

- A business plan is a document prepared by entrepreneurs, which summarises the future objectives of the proposed business and shows how they will be achieved.
- Entrepreneurs use a business plan to help raise money from banks and venture capitalists.

What does a Business Plan Contain?

The Business Idea

- A simple description of the purpose of the business and why the business will be a success.

Business Aims and Objectives

- The long-term goals of the business and the medium- to short-term steps to get there.

Target Market

- The group of people that the business will sell to. Through market research a customer profile can be created.

Forecast Revenue, Cost and Profit

- Predictions for how much the business will make from selling its goods or services, its costs and potential profit.

Cash-flow Forecast

- Monthly inflows and outflows of the business. An entrepreneur can see when cash flow may be negative and think about borrowing money to cover these times.

Sources of Finance

- The amount of money required to start a business and where it will come from. Including money invested by the entrepreneur, how much will need to be borrowed and when.

Location

- The business's location and specific information about the area. Also what the business will need to set up in this location.

Marketing Mix

- Each element of the marketing mix will need to be explained.

Why is it Important to Have a Business Plan?

- Banks and other investors will want to see a business plan to determine whether the business has a good chance of being successful.
- Potential investors will look at the financial information to ensure the business will be able to pay back any money that is borrowed with interest.
- Writing a business plan forces entrepreneurs to think about every aspect of the business – this may highlight areas that need further consideration.
- It is a plan that entrepreneurs can refer to and ensure there is direction for the business.
- Costly mistakes can be avoided if the business is well planned out, e.g. if an entrepreneur is aware of the costs of raw materials, they can carefully budget and set prices accordingly.
- The legal responsibilities of the business can be researched and planned for using a business plan.
- The risk of failure is reduced if the business has a plan and clear aims and objectives.
- Although business plans are important, not all entrepreneurs write one, preferring instead to go with their gut instinct.

> **Key Point**
>
> A business plan is important to minimise the risk of failure and to help obtain finance.

> **Quick Test**
>
> 1. Name the essential elements of a business plan.
> 2. Why do banks and other lenders want to see a business plan?
> 3. How does a business plan help to reduce the risk of a business failing?

> **Key Word**
>
> business plan

1 Why could survival be a more appropriate objective for a new business rather than an established business? Justify your answer. [3]

....

....

....

....

2 What or who do social enterprises aim to benefit? [2]

....

....

3 List **three** different fixed costs a business could incur. [3]

....

....

....

4 In business, what does the term 'loss' mean? [2]

....

....

5 What does the term 'insolvent' mean? [2]

....

....

6 Give **two** examples of short-term finance for a business. [2]

....

....

7 Calculate profit using the information below.   [5]

> Selling price = £10
>
> Sales quantity = 100
>
> Fixed cost = £20
>
> Variable cost per unit = £5

8 Using the information in Question 8, calculate the break-even point in both level of output and level of sales.   [3]

9 Assess the value of using retained profit as a source of finance.   [3]

10 Outline **one** benefit of taking out a loan over using share capital.   [2]

1. What is the difference between a franchisee and a franchisor? [2]

2. Explain why a sole trader faces more risk than a shareholder in a private limited company. [3]

3. State **one** benefit of choosing to start up a partnership. [1]

4. What are the **five** factors that affect business location? [5]

5. Why is location important for businesses in the primary sector? [1]

6. Explain why a business may choose a location close to labour. [2]

7   List the **four** elements of the marketing mix.   [4]

....

....

....

8   Explain what is meant by place and the options a business has to get products to customers.   [4]

....

....

....

9   How has technology made an impact on the place element of the marketing mix?   [3]

....

....

....

10 What is the purpose of a business plan?   [1]

....

11 Name **three** items that will be included in a business plan.   [3]

....

....

....

12 How does a business plan help to reduce risk when starting up a business?   [3]

....

....

....

Business Stakeholders

You must be able to:

- Identify who business stakeholders are and their different objectives
- Understand the role of stakeholders in a small business and how they can impact on the business
- Explain how stakeholders can often experience conflict.

What is a Stakeholder?

- A **stakeholder** is:
  - any person who has an interest in a business
  - any person who is affected by the activities of a business
  - any person who works for a business
  - any person who supplies a business
  - any person who competes with a business
  - any person who lives in the neighbourhood of a business
  - pressure groups who campaign against the activities of a business
  - any person who buys from a business or is the **end user** of its products.
- Internal stakeholders are people inside the business such as owners, management and employees.
- External stakeholders are people outside the business such as customers, suppliers and banks.

Internal Stakeholders

- **Owners** want profits, a good reputation and the potential to grow the business.
- **Managers** want good salaries, recognition for achieving targets and career success.
- **Employees** want good working conditions, a decent wage and job security.

External Stakeholders

- **Shareholders** want a return on their investment in **dividend** payouts.
- **Suppliers** want to sell their products at the highest price and be paid on time.
- **Customers** want to buy quality and reliable goods and services at the lowest price.
- The **local community** wants local investment, jobs and limited pollution.
- **Government** wants low unemployment, competitive markets and businesses to operate within the law and pay taxes.
- Banks want to lend money to businesses with limited risk of losing it.
- **Pressure groups** want to ensure businesses are acting ethically and are not polluting the environment.

> **Key Point**
>
> Do not confuse **stake**holders with **share**holders.

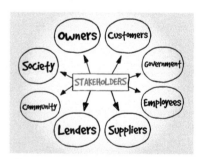

The Influence of Stakeholders

- Stakeholders can both influence a business or be influenced by the activities of a business.
- Owners make decisions that can influence the success of their business, e.g. deciding to open a new shop to expand the business: choosing the right location is critical.
- Employees can influence a business by providing excellent customer service, which helps to boost the reputation of the business. On the other hand, staff with poor customer service skills can drive away customers.
- Suppliers can influence a business by supplying it with goods of excellent quality, which can lead to repeat purchase by the business's customers. However, if supplies are of poor, or even dangerous quality, customers may choose in the future to buy goods elsewhere so the business and its suppliers lose custom.

Stakeholder Conflict

- Often stakeholders have different aims, which can cause stakeholder conflict, causing them to pull in different directions.
- This is because stakeholders do not always make decisions which are in the best interests of a business, instead they often aim to satisfy their own interests.

For example:

- the owner of a business may want to pay its workers the lowest wages in order to keep costs down so that customers can benefit from lower prices;
- however, if workers are paid low wages they are more likely to be dissatisfied, which might lead to low productivity, poor quality of work and resignations;
- therefore the business owner will need to balance the needs of profit with the desire for quality, motivated staff; some form of compromise will need to be made which best satisfies the owner, customers and workers.

> **Key Point**
>
> Stakeholders may have conflicting interests.

> **Key Words**
>
> stakeholders
> end user
> owners
> managers
> employees
> shareholders
> dividend
> suppliers
> customers
> local community
> government
> pressure groups
> stakeholder conflict

> **Quick Test**
>
> 1. Explain the term 'stakeholder'.
> 2. Explain three examples of 'external stakeholders'.
> 3. Explain what 'stakeholder conflict' is and give one example to support your answer.

Technology and Business

You must be able to:

- Explain different types of technology used by businesses
- Explain how technology influences business activity.

Technology and Sales

- Technology has brought e-commerce, which is buying and selling goods and services online.
- E-commerce makes it possible for businesses to sell at any time of day, so businesses can make continuous sales.
- E-commerce has made it possible for businesses to attract new customers from around the world.
- E-commerce has created a larger marketplace for businesses, which has helped increase sales.
- Technology has brought new payment systems (the electronic ability to transfer money quickly and safely from one bank account to another) such as PayPal, bringing time efficiency for customers.
- Businesses are now able to take orders online and deliver goods to customers' homes in a very short period of time.

Technology and Costs

- Keeping costs to a minimum is vital for any business and through the use of technology, businesses are now able to compare the prices of suppliers quickly and easily to find the cheapest suppliers.
- Many business startups use e-commerce without the need to find physical premises; this helps reduce overheads.
- To create a website and PayPal account is cheap and simple, so it is possible for one person to open and run a business without the need to hire technical staff.
- New technologies tend to remove the need for old machinery, or even human work, which has reduced costs, e.g.
  - Amazon relies more on robots in its warehouses than human workers
  - it's possible for Amazon's robots to function on a 24-hour basis, which humans are unable to do, thus reducing Amazon's operational costs.
- Businesses now use digital communication such as emails, texts and websites to communicate with different stakeholders; this is quick, efficient and cheap.
- Many businesses use biometrics to reduce time and increase efficiency and security, e.g. fingerprint scanning, iris scanning.

> ### Key Point
>
> Technology has provided businesses with more opportunities to sell to customers. It has also made business more competitive with prices.

Technology and the Marketing Mix

- The marketing mix is a blend of four elements: product, place, price and promotion.

Product

- Businesses are becoming more innovative with goods and services to keep up with changes in technology.
- Some goods have revolutionised certain industries, e.g. digital photography and Instagram.
- Some services have been created thanks to technology, e.g. Uber spotted an opportunity to use apps to bring customers and drivers together to remove the need for traditional taxi firms in some cities.
- In order to keep pace with technology and consumer demand, businesses have to continue innovating their goods and services.

Place

- Before e-commerce, business activities were more restricted – to buy goods and services, customers needed to visit shops.
- Shops had restricted opening hours, which meant customers could only buy goods and services when the shops were open.
- Websites are fast becoming the new 'place' to trade.
- Smartphones provide customers with portable access to the Internet, which has increased their opportunities to instantly buy products.

Price

- Technology has brought more efficiency in costs and time, which has enabled some businesses to reduce the prices of the goods they sell.
- Customers can now compare prices using price-comparison websites, which in turn has encouraged businesses to reduce prices in order to remain competitive.

Promotion

- Technology has made promotion quicker and cheaper for many businesses due to advancements in communication such as texts, emails and video calling, e.g. Skype.
- Social media has provided an effective way of promoting products via online campaigns.
- Viral marketing encourages consumers and the public to use social media to share information about a business's goods and services, e.g Netflix.

Key Point

Technology affects all areas of the marketing mix: product, place, price and promotion.

Key Words

e-commerce
sales
payment systems
costs
digital communication
biometrics
social media
viral marketing

Quick Test

1. Explain what e-commerce is and how it affects business.
2. Explain how technology has influenced prices.
3. Explain how technology influences the marketing mix.

Legislation and Business

You must be able to:

- Explain the purpose of legislation
- Discuss the impact that employment legislation and consumer legislation has on business.

Legislation, and Why it is Important

- **Legislation** refers to laws set by governments of countries.
- Legislation sets out a strict set of rules in which businesses can operate that do not exploit staff or customers.
- No business can gain a cost advantage over another by avoiding implementing costly requirements due to legislation; therefore, legislation is fair to all businesses.

The Principles of Employment Law

- All workers are entitled to be free of **discrimination** in the workplace.
- Businesses must treat all job applicants and workers fairly regardless of gender, age, race, religion, disability, sexual preference, type of contract or stage of pregnancy.
- All workers are entitled to receive a minimum wage. The National Living Wage is slightly higher than the minimum wage. Without this legislation, it would be possible for businesses to pay workers as little as the business wanted.
- All workers are protected from working too many hours each week.
- Any worker with a young family is entitled to time off work to look after their family.
- The Health and Safety Act states all workers have the right to work in a safe environment.
- Businesses examine all work areas to ensure no member of staff comes to harm (known as risk assessment).
- If a business needs to reduce its staffing levels, it must provide staff with sufficient warning and pay them compensation (redundancy pay).

> **Key Point**
>
> You will not have to learn the names of specific laws but you will need to know the purpose of legislation and the impact it has on business.

The Principles of Consumer Law

- A customer is anyone who *buys* a product.
- Consumers are people who *use* products.
- The Consumer Rights Act states the right to a refund if goods or services are not:

a) **of satisfactory quality** – which means that goods or services shouldn't be faulty or damaged when the consumer receives them.
   - Goods should last a 'reasonable' length of time.
   - Customers don't have the right to a refund if they damage the goods themselves or knew about existing damage at the point of sale.

b) **fit for purpose** – which means the goods or service must be able to do what they were designed to do.

c) **as described** – which means the description must match the product being sold.

- Goods and services must be correctly packaged and clearly labelled with correct measurements so customers are not deceived by any description.
- However, customers do not have a right to a refund if the goods or services are described correctly but a customer changes their mind after they have made the purchase.

Business and Complying with the Law

- If a business is caught breaking the law, it is likely to be heavily fined.
- If a business is caught breaking the law the owners or key staff may also be given prison sentences.
- By complying with the law businesses can avoid financial penalties or jail sentences.
- If customers learn of a business breaking the law, they may be disgusted and decide to never shop there again, which will affect future sales.
- A business should want to obey the law in order to maintain a good reputation, which helps future sales.

Changes in legislation

> **Quick Test**
>
> 1. Explain the purpose of legislation.
> 2. Name **two** areas of employment law a business must comply with.
> 3. Explain the **three** areas of consumer law that businesses need to obey.

> **Key Words**
>
> legislation
> discrimination
> customer
> consumer

The Economy and Business

You must be able to:

- Understand the impact of the economic climate on business
- Be able to discuss how changing levels of income affect consumer spending.

Economic Climate

- **Economic climate** refers to the broad performance of an economy.
- The economy is measured by **Gross Domestic Product (GDP)**, which is an estimate of the total value of goods and services produced in a country.
- The more the country produces, the stronger the economy is, and the healthier the economic climate.

Changing Levels of Consumer Income

- **Consumer income** is the amount of money consumers have left to spend after they have paid their taxes and living expenses.
- When consumer income rises, people tend to have more money, which leads to higher levels of consumer spending.
- Consumers tend to buy more expensive goods and services (luxuries) when they have lots of money.
- When consumer income reduces, people are not earning as much money so may spend less money or buy cheaper (inferior) products.

Unemployment and Business

- **Unemployment** has different impacts on the economy.

When unemployment is low	When unemployment is high
More workers are employed.	There are not enough jobs for people who are willing to work.
People have higher consumer income.	People have less consumer income.
Consumers spend more money.	Consumers spend less money.
Demand for luxury goods and services increases.	Demand for inferior goods and services increases.
Businesses produce more luxury products.	Businesses produce more inferior products.
Businesses hire more staff.	Businesses stop hiring and begin to make workers redundant.
There is a shortage of quality staff.	There is a surplus of quality staff.
Increased revenue and profit for businesses.	Decreased revenue and profit for businesses.
The government receives more tax and pays out less in benefits.	The government receives less tax and pays out more in benefits.

Other Factors that Affect Businesses and Consumer Income

Factor	Definition	When high	When low
Corporation Tax	A tax government charges to businesses based on a percentage of their profits.	Business costs increase and prices tend to increase.	Business costs decrease and prices tend to decrease.
Value Added Tax (VAT)	A tax added on top of selling prices for goods and services (or businesses whose turnover is more than £83 000 (2017)).	The price of goods and services increases.	The price of goods and services decreases.
Income tax	A tax paid to the government by individuals, based on their annual income.	Less consumer income.	More consumer income.
Inflation	Inflation is when the prices of goods and services continue to rise.	Higher costs for businesses and higher prices for consumers.	Lower costs for businesses and lower prices for consumers.
Interest rates (charged by banks as a result of the Bank Base Rate set by the Bank of England)	The cost of borrowing (and reward for saving) money is the interest rate.	The cost of borrowing increases for businesses and consumers, so their costs increase.	The cost of borrowing decreases for businesses and consumers, so their costs decrease.
Exchange rates	The cost of exchanging one currency for another is the exchange rate.	When the pound is high, imports are cheap (meaning more consumer income), exports are expensive.	When the pound is low, imports are expensive (meaning less consumer income), exports are cheap.

Quick Test

1. Explain what the term 'economic climate' means and how it is measured.
2. Explain how unemployment affects businesses.
3. Explain how high interest rates can affect consumer spending.

External Influences

You must be able to:

- Understand how businesses respond to changes in technology, legislation and economic climate.

Business Responses to Changes in Technology

- Many businesses now use computer-aided manufacturing (CAM), robots and 3D printing to replace or assist human labour.
- Shops and other provider services, such as restaurants, have Electronic Funds Transfer at Point of Sale (EFTPOS) which speed up transactions in shops by paying with bank cards; they also provide vital electronic data to help businesses maintain stock levels.
- Technology has changed the workplace as staff use more emails, video calls and websites.
- Technology is also being used for marketing purposes and many businesses recruit and train staff for telemarketing, which involves servicing and selling products to customers over the telephone.

The Benefits and Criticisms of Technology

- Technology has helped reduce running costs and wastage whilst increasing productivity, competitiveness, innovation, speed, accuracy.
- Technology costs money to buy, install, and train staff to use, maintain and replace.
- Technology has been criticised for job losses, loss of traditional skills and the demotivation of staff.

Legislation and Regulation

Legislation and regulation	Purpose
Employment laws	To ensure workers: work in a safe environment; receive fair wages; are treated equally; do not work too many hours; are treated fairly if made redundant.
Consumer Rights Act	The Consumer Rights Act is a law that protects consumer rights when buying products from businesses.
Trading Standards Authority (TSA)	The Trading Standards Authority (TSA) is a local government service that regulates and enforces to ensure the public is protected from businesses selling counterfeits (fakes), inaccurate measures and inaccurate weights of goods.

Advertising Standards Authority (ASA)	The Advertising Standards Authority (ASA) is the UK's independent advertising regulator that ensures all business advertising is accurate and true. It also deals with complaints from the public about advertising.
Environmental laws	Minimise risk to the environment and to the health of the public.
Tax laws	Ensure businesses are paying the correct taxes to the government.
Competition law	To ensure no businesses becomes dominant and that prices are fair.

Impact of the Economic Environment

- **Exchange rates** have a large impact on businesses that import or export.
- The acronym **SPICED** is useful to help remember:
  - when there is a **S**trong **P**ound, **I**mports are **C**heap, and **E**xports are **D**ear.
- **Interest rates** affect businesses too.
- When interest rates are high, businesses often find costs go up as it becomes expensive to borrow.
- When interest rates are high, businesses are less likely to invest.
- When interest rates are high, consumers with mortgages, loans and credit cards tend to have less income, so reduce their spending, which means fewer sales for businesses.
- When interest rates are low, consumers tend to have more money to spend.
- **Inflation** means a rise in prices.
- Inflation tends to be bad for business as it increases costs for businesses, reducing profits, unless businesses pass these costs on to their customers (which may lead to fewer sales).
- **Unemployment** affects the whole of business and society.
- When there is high unemployment, workers have less income, which means they are less likely to spend money.
- If workers buy less, businesses sell less, which can lead to some businesses struggling as their revenue declines (perhaps resulting in more redundancies).
- **Uncertainty** in the economic outlook affects consumers and businesses, e.g. the 2016 Brexit result will have an impact for years while the government, businesses and the UK public work out how leaving the European Union affects everyone.

> **Key Point**
>
> Strong
> Pound
> Imports
> Cheap
> Exports
> Dear

> **Key Words**
>
> Consumer Rights Act
> Trading Standards Authority (TSA)
> Advertising Standards Authority (ASA)

> **Quick Test**
>
> 1. How has technology changed the workplace?
> 2. What is the role of the Trading Standards Authority?
> 3. What is inflation?

1 Outline **one** disadvantage of a franchise to a franchisee. [1]

....

....

2 What is meant by the term 'liability'? [1]

....

3 Why is it important for an entrepreneur to consider which type of business to start? [2]

....

....

....

4 Why do some businesses choose to locate close to competitors? [1]

....

....

5 Why is location important for some businesses and not for others? [1]

....

....

6 Explain how the Internet has allowed businesses to save costs in regard to location. [2]

....

....

7 Explain why price is an important element of the marketing mix for businesses in a competitive market. [2]

....

....

....

8 How do customer needs impact the marketing mix? [3]

....

....

....

9 How has the Internet made an impact on the promotion element of the marketing mix?
Use examples in your answer. [2]

....

....

....

10 What is a business plan? [1]

....

....

11 Why is it important for an entrepreneur to include a cash-flow forecast in a business plan? [2]

....

....

....

12 How does a business plan help an entrepreneur understand their legal responsibilities? [2]

....

....

....

1. List **three** internal stakeholders. [3]

2. Explain how a supplier can influence a business. [3]

3. Explain how the aims of shareholders may differ to the aims of employees. [2]

4. List **three** ways in which technology can help a business reduce its costs. [3]

5. What does it mean when a business treats employees free of discrimination? [4]

6. What is a risk assessment? [1]

7   A consumer is entitled to buy products that are fit for purpose.
What does 'fit for purpose' mean?   [1]

8   What is consumer income?   [1]

9   Which type of businesses prosper from a recession?   [1]

10   What is Value Added Tax (VAT)?   [2]

11   What are exchange rates?   [1]

12   What is the aim of the Consumer Rights Act?   [2]

13   What is the role of the Trading Standards Authority?   [2]

Business Growth

You must be able to:

- Identify methods of business growth
- Know the types of business ownership for growing businesses
- Identify sources of finance for growing and established businesses.

Why Would a Business Want to Grow?

- If a business grows, it can:
  - benefit from economies of scale
  - which means being able to provide more goods or services, making it cheaper to make each product
  - benefit from a larger market share
  - gain more recognition, customers, revenue and profit.

Growing a Business

The following table details how to grow a business.

	Organic (internal) growth	Inorganic (external) growth
Definition	Organic growth is when a business grows on its own.	Inorganic growth is when a business combines with another business to grow.

How is it achieved?	Through changing the marketing mix by:
	• Taking existing products to new markets in the UK or overseas.
	• Developing new products via:
	  – research and development
	  – taking advantage of new technology
	  – innovation.
	• Becoming a public limited company (plc) by floating on the stock market (see below).
		Through a:
		• Merger (when two businesses join together) or
		• Takeover (when one business buys a smaller business).

Advantages	A business can maintain its own values without interference.	• Rapid growth. • New shared resources/skills/customers.
Disadvantages	Slower growth.	Disagreements and communication problems.

Finance Options for Growth

- Capital found from within a business is an internal source of finance.
- Capital found from outside a business is an external source of finance.

The table on the opposite page helps clarify these options.

> **Key Point**
>
> Inorganic growth (through merger with, or takeover of, another business) can speed business expansion.

Finance options	Advantages	Disadvantages
Internal source of finance		
• **Retained profits** – using capital from profits kept from previous years of trading.	Cheap, quick and convenient.	Might not have any retained profits or might need the funds for something else. Also, once the money is gone, not available for future unseen problems.
• Sale of **assets**, e.g. selling machinery or land.	Convenient, can create space for more profitable uses, can be quick.	Might not get the market value or even sell at all; might need the assets in the future. It also looks desperate.
• Owner's own savings.	Quick, convenient and cheap.	Might not have any savings or may need cash for private purposes.
External source of finance		
• **Loan capital** – lump sum of capital borrowed from a bank.	Regular repayments spread over a period of time assist with cash-flow management. Often a bank manager gives financial advice.	Can take a while to be approved; might not qualify; interest applies, so can be expensive. Often a bank will insist on collateral (security) being offered by a business in case the business fails to make loan repayments.
• **Share capital** (also known as share issue) – when a business becomes a private limited company by offering shares in the business in exchange for capital.	Does not need to be repaid; no interest applies; business can choose who to offer shares to.	Profits are paid to shareholders (known as dividends); control of the business is diluted.
• **Stock market floatation** – when a business becomes a public limited company by offering shares to the public to buy.	Can raise large amounts of capital as is easy for the public to buy shares via a stockbroker or bank; does not need to be repaid; no interest applies; business becomes more recognised.	Complicated and expensive; loss of control as anyone can buy shares; profits are paid to shareholders (dividends); business records are made public; some investors only buy shares to make a quick profit by selling them when the share price increases.

> **Key Words**
>
> economies of scale
> organic growth
> inorganic growth
> public limited company (plc)
> merger
> takeover
> internal source of finance
> external source of finance
> retained profits
> assets
> loan capital
> share capital
> stock market floatation

> **Quick Test**
>
> 1. Explain the difference between organic growth and inorganic growth.
> 2. Explain the benefits of internal finance for growth.
> 3. Explain the drawbacks of loan capital.

Changes in Business Aims and Objectives

You must be able to:

- Explain why business aims and objectives change as businesses evolve
- Explain how business aims and objectives change as businesses evolve.

Why Business Aims and Objectives Change as Businesses Evolve

- Aims are the long-term goals of a business.
- Objectives are the short-term steps a business takes to realise those goals.
- Over time, many businesses need to change their aims and objectives as the business evolves to adapt to changing circumstances.
- When businesses evolve, they may find market conditions change and they need to be able to respond to these changes, e.g. the growth rate of the market (whether the market is becoming bigger or smaller) or how competitive the market is.
- The economic climate may also have an effect on market conditions, which affects consumer income, and in turn their levels of spending.
- Consumer taste may change, e.g. an emphasis on recycling, which requires businesses to revisit their aims and objectives.
- New technology brings innovation and businesses find they need to change their aims and objectives to remain competitive.
- Often the previous performance of a business acts as a platform for setting new aims and objectives for the future – a successful business may change its aims and objectives to include future growth or a failing business will have to revisit its aims and objectives to include a change in direction, e.g. store closures and a renewed focus on website and deliveries instead.
- Legislation often causes businesses to change their aims and objectives, e.g. a change in the law regarding food labelling has encouraged many businesses to adopt aims and objectives which promote public health awareness.
- Sometimes business aims and objectives change in response to internal reasons, e.g. it could be that the original aim of the business is no longer applicable – when Marks & Spencer began in 1884 it was a penny bazaar stall, now it sells a wide range of goods and services nationally and internationally.

Key Point
Aims and objectives change over time.

How Aims and Objectives Change as Businesses Evolve

- Simple survival for a new business may change into the need to make a profit after its first year and to growth aims over a period of years.
- The business may have in its plans sales forecasts that require different aims and objectives for each year.
- A business may enter a new market to help it meet changed aims and objectives, e.g. Uber originally provided customers with the ability to call for transport when needed, now the business has entered the food home delivery market with UberEATS.
- Sometimes a business needs to exit a market to meet its aims and objectives, e.g. Tesco entered the American market but failed, this failure had a negative impact on their aims and objectives, so they decided to exit the US market.
- A business may need to change the size of its workforce over time to meet changing aims and objectives, e.g. the Post Office and many seasonal stores hire extra staff over the Christmas period to cope with extra customer demand for services.
- There may be times when a business has to reduce its workforce in order to meet its changing aims and objectives.
- Sometimes businesses need to change their product range to meet changed aims and objectives, e.g. many dairy farmers now produce cheese and yogurt products in addition to milk.
- Some businesses have reduced their product range to return to their core business in order to meet their aims and objectives,

> ### Key Point
>
> As technology evolves, many businesses need to change their aims and objectives to keep up with innovation

> ### Key Words
>
> market conditions
> legislation
> survival
> growth
> product range

Business and Globalisation

You must be able to:

- Understand the impact of globalisation on business
- Identify barriers to international trade
- Explain how businesses compete internationally.

Globalisation and Business

- **Globalisation** is when organisations and businesses trade internationally.
- **Exports** are when a business makes products in the UK then sells them to other countries.
- The UK's top exports are: pearls, gems, coins, oil and cars.
- Tourism is an export and is a major contributor to the UK economy.
- **Imports** are when products made overseas are brought into the UK.
- The top UK imports are: machines, vehicles and electronic equipment.

Changing Business Locations

- With globalisation, many UK businesses have relocated to low-cost locations overseas, e.g. Dyson vacuum cleaners are manufactured in Malaysia, where land and labour is cheaper.
- This type of relocation is known as offshoring; work is sent overseas to a host country that welcomes the operation of foreign businesses.
- Foreign businesses also locate to the UK to manufacture here, e.g. Nissan, the Japanese car company, has a plant in the UK because it wants to make the most of British skilled labour and to benefit from being closer to their European customers, so they do not need to transport their cars all the way from Japan.
- **Multinational companies (MNCs)** are businesses that operate and trade in more than one country.
- MNCs benefit from lower production costs by operating in developing countries and by being closer to their customers in the host countries in which they operate.
- MNCs can avoid import restrictions if they operate in host countries. Examples of MNCs are Coca-Cola and Pepsi.

Barriers to International Trade

- Many governments worry that cheap imports make it difficult for their own country's businesses to compete so they deliberately restrict opportunities, efficiency and competition for importers with trade barriers, such as tariffs.
- A tariff is a tax added onto the selling price of an imported good to make it more expensive to buy in the UK.
- If imported products are more expensive for UK consumers, they are less likely to want to buy them (reducing demand) and are more likely to buy UK products.
- If the UK imposes tariffs on imported goods, it often follows that governments of other countries also impose tariffs on UK exports entering their country, which makes it expensive for our businesses to export.
- Trade blocs are when certain countries group together to make it easier for members to market goods, services, capital, and labour by getting rid of all barriers to trade.
- Trade blocs tend to be close to one another geographically, e.g. the North American Free Trade Agreement (NAFTA), the European Union (EU).

How Businesses Compete Internationally

- Globalisation has created opportunities for Internet-based e-commerce businesses to sell to new markets; this means that businesses can use the Internet to buy and sell products anywhere in the world.
- Businesses do not even need to have their own websites or shops as they can use sites such as ebay to trade.
- Some businesses base their whole business model around e-commerce, such as Amazon.
- Websites even offer translation services so trading with consumers around the world becomes easier.
- Changes to the marketing mix can help a business to compete internationally, e.g. adaptation of products to suit local tastes, price amendments to take currencies into account, transportation arrangements, different promotional techniques.

> ### Key Point
>
> Tariffs are restrictions put in place by government to try to reduce cheap imports by making it more expensive and difficult for foreign countries to export to the UK.

> ### Quick Test
>
> 1. Explain the term 'globalisation'.
> 2. Explain the difference between imports trad exports.
> 3. Explain how tariffs can restrict imports.

> ### Key Words
>
> globalisation
> exports
> imports
> multinational companies (MNCs)
> trade barriers
> tariffs
> trade blocs
> e-commerce

Ethics, the Environment and Business

You must be able to:

- Discuss the impact of ethical and environmental considerations on businesses.

What are Ethics?

- **Ethics** are moral guidelines for good behaviour – doing what is morally right.
- When a business is ethical it pays a fair wage to its workers and ensures production does not harm the environment, animals or people.

Ethics, Environmental Considerations and Trade-offs

- High profits can conflict with ethics because businesses need to produce goods and services at a cost which is less than the price it charges customers.
- Many businesses have been accused of using very cheap labour without proper health and safety provisions to minimise costs in order to make as large a profit as possible.
- Brand names such as Primark have been in the news for paying foreign suppliers who hire children to sew clothes for hours on end. Primark found some UK customers began to **boycott** their stores as a protest, so the business needed to find a **trade-off** to resolve the situation.
- Trade-offs are a compromise between one thing and another.
- In the case of Primark, the company realised that they would need to regularly check that children are no longer used in the production of goods or change suppliers. This increased costs but Primark could see the benefit of this trade-off; Primark could still make a profit without exploiting children overseas.
- The environment should also be protected and business activities should be influenced to ensure that environmental considerations are made.
- Some businesses have been accused of helping to destroy the environment, e.g. firms who use palm oil in their products. The palm oil industry burns tropical rainforests to make room for new plantations; this practice threatens the orangutan population in places like Borneo. A trade-off for such business would be to buy palm oil from organisations who harvest palm oil using **sustainable** methods.

> ### Key Point
>
> Ethical business practices can add costs to businesses. However some businesses have found they sell more of their products by being ethical so any additional costs are outweighed by an increase in sales.

- Using sustainable methods costs more, which affects profit, but ethical businesses know they need to also help the environment if they want sustainable profits.

Ethics and the Reputation of a Business

- Some businesses see ethics as a form of added value to their goods and services, e.g. Lush.
- Companies who have acted in a non-ethical way have suffered criticism and drops in sales, e.g. Starbucks stores suffered when it was made public that Starbucks avoided paying UK taxes in full.

Pressure Group Activity and the Marketing Mix

- **Pressure groups** are groups of people who aim to influence government and public opinion over issues they feel strongly about in order to change laws or behaviour.
- Pressure groups influence companies to change by writing letters to MPs and the media, and by staging marches and publicity stunts, e.g. the Climate Group.
- The impact of pressure group activity can also influence businesses to change their marketing mix to adopt more ethical practices, e.g. below are some amendments made by UK supermarkets in response to pressure group activities:

  - **Products** – supermarkets have better checks in place with suppliers to ensure all meat ingredients are genuine and correctly labelled, following horsemeat scandals.
  - **Place** – sweets are no longer placed by checkout tills, as their placement was previously criticised as tempting children into pestering parents to buy them.
  - **Price** – Tesco no longer charge higher prices for 'female' coloured razors than 'male' coloured razors in a move to eliminate claims of sexist product pricing.
  - **Promotion** – supermarkets place covers over adult-aimed 'lads mags' so they are not promoted in their stores as a direct result of pressure groups complaining that such magazines can be seen by children, which is not ethical.

Quick Test

1. Explain the term 'ethics'.
2. Explain how ethics can conflict with profit.
3. Discuss how ethics can affect business.

Key Words

ethics
boycott
trade-off
sustainable
pressure groups

1 What is an external stakeholder? [2]

_____

_____

2 Explain how employees can influence a business. [3]

_____

_____

_____

3 Name **two** ways in which a local community is a stakeholder in a business. [2]

_____

_____

_____

4 How has technology influenced the product of the marketing mix? [2]

_____

_____

_____

5 What does the minimum wage protect workers from? [2]

_____

_____

6 List **three** things that employees are entitled to when working. [3]

_____

_____

_____

7 Explain **two** benefits of a business ensuring it complies with employment and consumer legislation. [6]

8 What tends to happen to consumers' buying habits when consumer income reduces? [2]

9 Bob was able to import 625 teddy bears for $8 each from America when the exchange rate was £1 = $1.25. How much did Bob have to pay for the bears in £? [2]

10 If the exchange rate increased to $1.75, what would be the overall impact for Bob? Calculation not necessary. [2]

11 Describe how a rise in interest rates can affect a business. [8]

1   Explain the term 'economies of scale'.   [2]

_____

_____

2   Explain the benefits for a business of growing inorganically.   [3]

Businesses that grow inorganically have the
advantage of not needing to train new
staff which would take up time and money to
do so.

3   What does 'stock market flotation' mean?   [1]

When a business becomes a PLC by offering shares
to the public

4   What is the difference between aims and objectives?   [2]

_____

_____

5   Give an example of when a business may need to revisit aims and objectives it has
    made in the past.   [1]

_____

_____

6   What does the term 'offshoring' mean?   [2]

This is moving changing business location
where it's cheaper.

7   What does the term 'trade barrier' mean?   [1]

_____

8 What is a trade bloc? [3]

A trade bloc is when countries group together to make it easier for members to trade by getting ride of trade barriers.

9 Give an example of how a business can act ethically. [1]

Pay their workers a fair wage.

10 What does the term 'sustainability' mean? [2]

Sustainability

11 Explain how a business may benefit from being ethical. [3]

12 Name **two** ways in which a business can grow inorganically. [2]

Business takeover

Merge

13 Explain why retained profit might not always be a suitable source of finance for business growth. [3]

You don't get help from anyone but also is a big risk as it's personal savings

Product

You must be able to:

- Understand the different elements of the design mix
- Explain the phases of the product life cycle and how businesses use extension strategies
- Discuss the importance to a business of differentiating a good/service.

Design Mix

- A product can be a good or service.
- To achieve a successful product design, a business will concentrate on three elements that make up the design mix: function, appearance (aesthetics) and cost.

Function

- Function is about the capabilities of the product; can it perform its intended purpose? For example, will a waterproof jacket keep a customer dry?
- Focusing on functionality can make products unique, e.g. the 'AddWash' feature on some washing machines allows customers to add items to the washing machine while the cycle is in operation.
- For medical equipment, functionality takes priority over design as the equipment must perform a specific purpose.

Appearance (aesthetics)

- Aesthetics is about the look, taste or feel of a product. If the product is stylish, elegant and attractive, the chances are that it will appeal to customers and sell well.

Cost

- Businesses should produce a product as cost effectively as possible – this can lead to a competitive advantage being gained.
- High production costs lead to higher selling prices and may prevent customers buying products.
- The importance of cost is connected to the nature of the product – if a business has a focus on high quality, it will incur higher production costs.

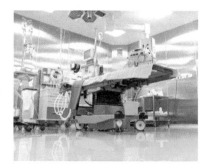

Product Life Cycle

- The product life cycle maps the stages a product passes through over time and the sales that can be expected from that stage.
- It can be shown in graph form and consists of the introduction phase, growth phase, maturity phase, and decline phase.
- A business can map their full product range on a product life cycle graph and determine which products need more focus.

Key Point

The importance of the three elements of the design mix will depend on the nature of the product.

- The **introduction phase** comprises product launch.
  - Initial research, design and development will mean costs are high.
  - Sales will be low as customers are unaware that the product is for sale.
  - Businesses spend money on promotion.
  - As costs are high and sales are low, it is likely that no profit is made at this stage.
- The **growth phase** sees sales grow as awareness and popularity are increased.
  - Sales grow with demand and the business may start to make a profit.
- The **maturity phase** sees sales peak.
  - Growth of sales may slow down due to other businesses joining the market.
  - Profit may be high but start to reduce.
- The **decline phase** may see products become out-dated as tastes and technology change.
  - Sales and profits fall and a business may have to consider if they want to continue selling the product.
- A business will try and prevent a product going into the decline phase by using extension strategies. This can be achieved by making changes to the product (e.g. lower price) or by appealing to a new segment of the market.

Product Life Cycle

Product Differentiation

- Depending on the nature of the product, a business will choose to either focus on function, aesthetics or cost to meet their customer needs and to achieve product differentiation.
- Product differentiation can be created using the following:
  - brand image
  - unique selling point/s
  - offering a better location, features, function, design appearance
  - cheaper selling price
  - quality
  - customer service
  - product range.

Key Words

design mix
product life cycle
introduction phase
growth phase
maturity phase
decline phase
extension strategies
product differentiation

Quick Test

1. What are the three elements of the design mix?
2. How do businesses extend the life cycle of their products?
3. Name three ways a business can achieve product differentiation.

Price

You must be able to:

- Explain the different methods used by businesses to price their products
- Discuss influences on pricing strategies.

Price

- **Price** is the amount that customers pay for a product.
- Price is an important decision for businesses as it is directly linked to revenue.
- A business needs to carefully consider their **pricing strategy**, and this is based on a number of factors.

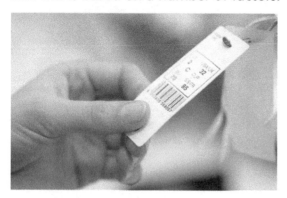

Pricing Strategies

- Businesses may set a low price when a product first enters the market, to encourage people to buy it, and raise the price later.
- A business will decide on a price to reflect the brand and quality of their product.
- A business may consider their profit margins when deciding on a pricing strategy.
- A high price may be set for a new product that is innovative or has special features, often from a well-known brand. Some customers will be attracted to the desire to be part of a premium market; the higher price increases profit.
- Price can be set in line with competitors so customers have to make decisions on which products to buy based on other factors, such as quality or appearance.

Profit Margins

- Profit margin is the difference between the sale price and the cost of production – a low profit margin means a business has to sell a large volume of products to make a profit, as the selling price is close to the cost of making the product.
- A business that operates at high profit margins generally sells fewer products than one operating at low profit margins.

- Businesses that operate at high profit margins sell products for a price that is much higher than the cost of production so they do not need to rely on a large volume of sales to make a profit.

Influences on Pricing Strategies

Technology

- **Freemium** is a pricing strategy used mainly for digital products, such as software, media or gaming, that are offered for free. Money (premium) then has to be paid if a user wants additional features, functionality or virtual goods, e.g. Candy Crush.
- Customers can easily compare prices on comparison websites and businesses need to ensure that their prices are in line with competitors.
- Technology has led to better machinery or tools, which means that businesses can make their goods quicker or provide a quicker service, which in turn saves costs and increases profit for the business, e.g. a taxi company uses satellite navigation that provides traffic updates and fast route options.

Competition

- Operating in a competitive environment can drive a business to reduce their pricing to remain competitive in the market.
- If a business sells a product with little differentiation, e.g. water, they will have to keep prices similar to their competitors.

Market Segments

- A business must consider the ability of their target customers to pay for their products.
- If the target market is price-sensitive, then demand will fall if the business charges a price that is too high.

Product Life Cycle

- Introduction and growth: price helps to determine the value of a product, push sales or recover development and promotion costs.
- Maturity: price can be used to maintain profit margins or in a competitive market a business may set their price to be in line with competitors to maintain their market share.
- Decline: price helps to encourage sales when customers are not prepared to pay a high amount.

Key Point

Price is linked to product (see pages 76–77) as different methods of pricing are relevant for each stage of the product life cycle.

> **Quick Test**
>
> 1. Describe **one** pricing strategy a business may use to price its products.
> 2. How does technology influence pricing strategies?
> 3. Why might a product be priced differently during the introduction stage compared to the decline stage of its life cycle?

Key Words

price
pricing strategy
freemium

Promotion

You must be able to:

- Discuss how businesses use appropriate promotion strategies to target different market segments
- Explain how businesses use technology in promotion.

Promotion

A **promotion strategy** is when a business carefully identifies how to get the right message at the right time in the right way to its **market segment**.

- The preferences of the market segment are fundamental to the promotion strategy.
- A business will use one or a mix of the following promotion strategies:

  - advertising
  - sponsorship
  - product trials
  - special offers
  - branding.

> ### Key Point
>
> Businesses need to use the appropriate promotion strategy to suit their desired market segment.

Promotion Strategies for Different Market Segments

Advertising

- A business can advertise on TV, radio, magazines and newspapers, billboards, websites, emails, through apps and many other channels.
- Advertising can target a large number of people at the same time.
- TV advertising may be more effective for the older generation.
- Younger viewers often watch TV on demand, which limits advertising, requiring businesses to advertise to this group differently. For example, more interactive adverts on social media.

Sponsorship

Sponsorship involves a business financially supporting or giving goods or services to an event or programme in return for advertising their brand.

- A business must use relevant events or programmes to reach their market segment and develop their brand.

Product Trials

- **Product trials** are used to get customers to try a product for the first time, usually before a business decides to launch it fully to the market.
- A large established restaurant chain may offer a new dish on their menu in restaurants located in a particular area as a way of testing a product.

Special Offers

- Can take the form of a discount on the sales price, e.g. a complementary deal.
- A business targeted at a specific segment of the market (niche market), for example, vegan snacks, might offer a free product if a friend is recommended.
- A business that sells products with a mass appeal (mass market), e.g. fruit juices, might offer 'buy one get one free'.

Branding

A business can differentiate itself from other similar products using an image or identity that creates a unique brand.

- Customers can grow loyal to a branded business and trust it.
- A branded business charges higher prices as customers are willing to pay more.

The Use of Technology in Promotion

- Targeted advertising online allows businesses to direct promotion to their customers through email offers, pop-ups and banner adverts.
- Online advertising can be targeted because browsing habits are collected through Internet cookies and used by businesses to tailor their advertising to Internet users, e.g. if a user regularly looks at sports-related items, the user will see more adverts for trainers, game tickets etc., even when they are on a website that has nothing to do with sport.
- The success of an online advertising campaign can be measured using the click-through rate.
- Viral advertising relies on consumers passing on a promotion or advert via email or social media, which means it must grab the consumer's attention.
- E-newsletters are newsletters that are sent to customers via email and they can be interactive and captivating. Web-links allow customers to respond easily.

> ### Key Point
>
> Businesses can use technology to enhance their promotions through targeted advertising online, viral advertising via social media, and e-newsletters.

> ### Quick Test
>
> 1. State how a business may adapt their advertising to target younger generations.
> 2. How can a business use a special offer to target a mass market product?
> 3. Name **one** way a business can use technology to promote their business.

> ### Key Words
>
> promotion strategy
> market segment
> product trial
> brand
> Internet cookies
> click-through rate
> viral advertising
> e-newsletter

Place

You must be able to:

- Understand the importance of place in the marketing mix
- Explain how goods and services can be distributed using retailers, e-tailers.

What is Place?

- **Place** refers to the location where customers can purchase goods and services.
- To have a successful marketing mix, a business needs to ensure their products are available in the right place at the right time for customers to purchase.
- The route that a product takes, from where it is manufactured, to where it is sold, is called the **distribution channel**.
- Most goods and services in the UK are distributed through retailers or e-tailers.

Key Point

In the UK, goods and services are mainly distributed through retailers and e-tailers.

Retailers

- **Retailers** are the 'middle men' – they buy large quantities of products from a **manufacturer** or a wholesaler and make the products available locally to customers.
- Retailers have a physical location for customers to visit and purchase products.
- Retailers make purchasing products convenient for their customers – they add value to the products, e.g. free parking, product warranty, customer service.
- Adding value means the retailer can charge a higher price for the product and this is how they make a profit.
- As a retailer buys a large quantity of products, the price per unit will be cheaper; this reduces the profit margins for the manufacturer but allows the retailer to add their own mark-up.
- Retailers can take the form of: independent retailers (small shops), supermarkets, department stores, market traders, or multiples (a chain of stores).

E-tailers

- **E-tailers** are businesses that sell goods and services through the Internet.
- Some e-tailers are online-only e-tailers, such as Amazon.

- Other businesses use both e-tailing and retailing to sell their products, e.g. Argos.
- **E-commerce** involves electronic transactions via the Internet or electronic payment systems, e.g. contactless payments, bank cards, PayPal.
- E-tailers use e-commerce to create an online marketplace for customers. E-tailers have a global reach and allow customers the ability to shop at any time, wherever they are.
- As transactions take place over the Internet, businesses can track customers' buying habits to collect valuable market research.
- Small independent retailers or startup businesses can benefit from using large e-tailers to distribute their products.
- E-tailers must ensure they have: user-friendly websites to attract customers, regularly updated content – to meet changing customer needs – and **distribution** needs to be efficient, so customers can receive their orders quickly.
- It is expensive to set up e-tailing websites and customers may be reluctant to purchase over the Internet, due to fraud.

Quick Test

1. Why is 'place' important in the marketing mix?
2. What is the difference between a retailer and an e-tailer?
3. How do retailers make a profit?
4. How do e-tailers make purchasing goods and services more convenient for customers?
5. Why is it important for an e-tailer to have efficient distribution methods?

Key Words

place
distribution channel
retailer
manufacturer
e-tailer
e-commerce
distribution

Using the Marketing Mix to Make Business Decisions

You must be able to:

- Explain how each element of the marketing mix can influence the other elements
- Understand how businesses use the marketing mix to build a competitive advantage
- Discuss how an integrated marketing mix can influence competitive advantage.

Each Element of the Marketing Mix can Influence the Other Elements

Product

- Price – customers may demand a low-priced product so a business will need to produce their product cheaply, which will result in a lower quality product.
- Promotion – part of the promotion strategy may include changing the packaging of a product to make it more appealing to customers.
- Place – technology has led to customers changing where and when they demand their products. This has led to a change in the format of products, e.g. books are now available as e-books.

Price

- Product – strong brands and premium quality products will have higher prices.
- Promotion – special offers and discounts can reduce the price charged for a product.
- Place – an Internet-based business can charge a lower price because it doesn't have to pay costs associated with having premises.

Promotion

- Product – the life cycle of the product may influence the promotion used for it. Often when a product is new it will require lots of promotion, in contrast to the maturity stage when promotion takes place less often.
- Price – a high-priced, high-quality product will be promoted differently to a cheaper product. Buy-one, get-one-free can be used for cheaper products. Yet a high quality brand may focus on public relations.
- Place – e-tailers and high street retailers operate in a competitive environment and so offer a variety of promotions to attract customers, e.g. free delivery.

Place

- Product – the nature of the product will affect where it can be sold, e.g. a hairdresser is limited to where they can offer their services.
- Price – high-priced items, such as an exclusive brand of jewellery, will be only available at exclusive stores.
- Promotion – heavy promotion will mean a product needs to be available at more locations and for an extended time, e.g. Black Friday generally means longer opening hours and a larger number of products in stock.

Marketing Mix and Competitive Advantage

- **Competitive advantage** is an advantage held by a business that allows it to perform better than its competitors.
- Innovative goods or services exceed customer needs and allow a business to gain a competitive advantage, e.g. Uber, which allows users to request cars to their exact location using an app.
- New technology or buying cheaper raw materials reduces the cost of production and allows a business to sell its products more cheaply, creating a competitive advantage.
- Effective promotion can create a competitive advantage.
- Dispatching orders quickly, offering excellent after-sales care, being available in locations and times convenient to customers can provide great customer satisfaction, repeat purchases and possible competitive advantage.

Integrated Marketing Mix Influences Competitive Advantage

- Developing the correct balance between the elements of the marketing mix is important to build a successful marketing strategy and develop a competitive advantage.
- The correct blend of product, price, promotion and place depends on: the business's objectives, the market, the size of a business, the competition, the nature of the product.

> **Key Point**
>
> To gain a competitive advantage a business will need to use a combination of elements in the marketing mix.

> **Quick Test**
>
> 1. There is one right marketing mix that works for all businesses at all times. True or false?
> 2. How does the price of a product influence promotion? Use an example in your answer.
> 3. How can a business gain a competitive advantage though the product element of the marketing mix?

> **Key Word**
>
> competitive advantage

1 How can a business benefit from increased market share? [3]

2 What does the term 'merger' mean? [2]

When two business are merge to become one.

3 Describe what share capital is. [4]

Share capital is when a business becomes a privet limited company offering shares in the business for money.

4 Why might a change in consumer taste mean a business may need to change its aims and objectives? [2]

5 What sort of objective could a business that aims to grow implement? [1]

6 Why might a foreign business want to locate production in the UK? [3]

7 Why might the UK government impose import restrictions? [2]

....

8 How could a business change its marketing mix to suit a global market? [4]

....

....

....

....

9 Give **two** examples of poor working conditions for some workers whose employers do not have good ethics. [2]

....

....

10 What could be some consequences for a business that has not acted ethically? [3]

....

....

....

11 How can pressure groups influence change? [2]

....

....

....

1. What is meant by appearance (aesthetics)? [1]

This is the look, tast of feel of a product

2. Explain what is happening with sales, growth and profit during the maturity stage of a product life cycle. [3]

→Peak.
Growth is a stage where the product having and increase in sales and revenu as it is new. Maturity is when growth slows down.

3. Give **one** example of a pricing strategy a business may use to set their prices. [1]

A business may set there price low so people will by buy it and rais the price later.

4. Explain **one** way technology has influenced pricing decisions for businesses. [2]

Technology has influenced prices as people can easily compare prices with the compertition so they have to make sure they are on the same level.

5. Why does a business need to consider their target market when making pricing decisions? [2]

Customers must be able to afford the product but if it's to low people

6. Define promotion strategy. [1]

When a business carefully identifies how a to get the right message, to the right person at the right time.

7 State **two** ways a business can use technology to promote its goods and services. [2]

Adverts

Viral advertising

8 How does place contribute to a successful marketing mix? [1]

9 Name **one** benefit of using e-newsletters. [1]

You can link websites making it easy fre for people to acasses the website

10 Give **one** disadvantage of being an e-tailer. [1]

It's expensive to set up a e-tailer website.

11 What is meant by competitive advantage? [1]

An advantage a business has over others which lets it perform better

12 How does the product element of the marketing mix influence the element of price? [3]

Business Operations

You must be able to:

- State the purpose of business operations
- Identify and explain the different production processes: job, batch and flow production
- Analyse the impact of the different production processes on businesses
- Discuss the impacts of technology on production.

Production Processes

- The purpose of production is to create goods and services.
- As a business grows, the owners will need to consider the most efficient way of organising production, to produce their products.

Job Production

- Job production is where one individual product is made at a time by one or a group of workers.
- Examples include: tailoring, the 2012 Olympic Stadium (now called the London Stadium).

Advantages	Disadvantages
• High quality and unique products that are tailored to meet customer needs • Higher prices demanded • Workers are motivated, as they are involved in all stages of production	• Highly skilled workers required, needing training and careful management • Lengthy production process and higher production costs per unit

Batch Production

- Batch production is where similar items are grouped and made together (in batches), e.g. brown bread, white bread.
- Equipment can be easily altered to make different batches.
- Workers focus on one area of the production process.

Advantages	Disadvantages
• Variety and choice for customers • Workers become skilled in the production area, less supervision is required • More products made at once • Materials required will be purchased in bulk, so business can save on costs (economies of scale, which means the greater the quantity of materials purchased, the lower the per-unit cost, creating savings for the business)	• Demotivated workers as a result of performing the same tasks • A delay in one batch can affect the production of another batch

Flow Production

- **Flow production** is where a large number of identical products are made on an assembly line.
- Production is automated, often with extensive machinery, technology and robotics in large factories.
- Products can be made in large numbers in a short space of time.
- Examples: cars, bottled drinks.

Advantages	Disadvantages
• Raw materials are purchased in bulk, so they are cheaper, saving money for the business (economies of scale) • Goods can be produced in large quantities, unit costs are lower • Production can be in process 24/7 without the need for breaks and holidays; quality is also improved	• Expensive to set up and buy factory, machinery and the technology required • Difficult to adapt production lines • Repetitive work leads to demotivated workers • A breakdown in one of the lines, affects the entire production process

The Impacts of Technology on Production

- Lower costs – in the short term, investment is high. Machinery and factory set up is expensive. In the long-term, cost savings will come from lower labour costs, improved quality so less wastage.
- Increased productivity – machines and robots work autonomously, unlike workers who need breaks, holidays and time off.
- Improved quality – computer aided design (CAD) is precise and machinery and robots reduce mistakes that can be made by human error.
- Further flexibility – computer aided manufacture (CAM) allows for adjustment in processes to make a variety of products, providing more flexibility for businesses and more choice for customers.

Key Point

Technology is changing the way in which businesses produce their products. The main impacts are to costs, productivity, quality and flexibility.

Key Words

goods
services
job production
production process
batch production
flow production
productivity
computer aided design (CAD)
computer aided manufacture (CAM)

Quick Test

1. What is the purpose of business operations?
2. What are the **three** production processes?
3. Name **four** impacts of technology on production.

Working with Suppliers

You must be able to:

- Interpret bar gate stock graphs and explain just in time (JIT), to understand how businesses manage stock
- Understand the factors which lead to the efficient procurement of raw materials
- Discuss the impact of logistics and supply decisions on: costs, reputation and customer satisfaction.

Stock

- **Stock** constitutes the materials a business holds for use in production or sales. Stock is also referred to as inventory.
- Stock can be: raw materials waiting to be used in the production process, stocks of materials that are not completed (work in progress) and finished goods.

Bar Gate Stock Graphs

- A business can manage their stocks by setting maximum, minimum and re-order levels of stock, displayed on a bar gate stock graph.
- The x-axis on the graph shows time in weeks, the y-axis shows the unit of stock.
- **Maximum stock level** – the largest amount of stock that the business will hold at any one time.
- **Minimum stock level (buffer stock)** – the lowest amount of stock that a business will hold at any one time.
- The minimum stock level allows a business to continue production if there were to be a delay in delivery or an unexpected order.
- **Re-order level** – the stock level where new stock will be ordered.
- **Lead time** – the time it takes for new stock to arrive once it has been ordered.
- **Order quantity** – the number of units ordered.
- The size of an order is the difference between the maximum stock level and the minimum stock level.

Just In Time (JIT)

- **Just in time (JIT)** stock management is where businesses do not hold any stock; raw materials and components are ordered exactly when they are needed and used straight away in the production process.
- JIT requires regular deliveries, which increases costs and requires strong supplier relationships.

> **Key Point**
>
> Students will not have to draw a bar gate stock graph in the exam.

INVENTORY CONTROL

> **Key Point**
>
> Lead time is the difference between the re-order level (in weeks) and the minimum stock level (in weeks).

- Good cash-flow can be achieved as money is not tied up in stock or storage costs.
- However, economies of scale can't be utilised as raw materials are not bought in bulk.
- Supplier difficulties or a delay in delivery halts production and this can be costly for the business.

Efficient Procurement of Raw Materials

- Procurement is the act of obtaining or buying raw materials, components or services from a supplier to be used in the production of goods and services.
- Businesses need to maintain a good relationship with their suppliers. When choosing a supplier, a business will need to consider the following factors:
  - **quality** – a business needs the best quality raw materials or services for the best price
  - **delivery** – suppliers should be reliable, deliver on time, at short notice and with reasonable delivery costs
  - **availability** – suppliers need to have stock or components available when a business orders
  - **cost** – a business must negotiate prices to make cost savings and will want favourable payment terms
  - **trust** – suppliers want to be treated fairly and paid on time. Honest communication and joint problem solving will develop the trust between a supplier and a business.

The Impact of Logistics and Supply Decisions

- A business needs to ensure careful planning goes into decisions about their logistics and suppliers.
- A reliable supplier may be more expensive and increase costs for a business, however a business can rest assured that they'll be able to meet their demand and produce good quality products for their customers. This ensures customer satisfaction and a good reputation for the business and its brand.
- Distance between factories and a supplier needs careful planning – being in close proximity to suppliers means delivery times are not too long and allows for flexibility should unexpected orders need to be made.

Key Words

stock
bar gate stock graph
maximum stock level
minimum stock level
  (buffer stock)
re-order level
lead time
order quantity
just in time (JIT)
procurement
logistics

Quick Test

1. State the elements shown on a bar gate stock graph.
2. Define just in time stock control.
3. Name the **five** factors that a business should consider when choosing a supplier.

Managing Quality

You must be able to:

- Define quality
- Explain the difference between quality control and quality assurance
- Discuss the importance of managing quality in allowing a business to control costs and gain a competitive advantage.

Quality

- **Quality** is about meeting a minimum set of standards to satisfy customer expectations for a good or service.
- As markets become more competitive, customer demands increase.
- The rise of technology has led to customers sharing information about goods and services and leaving negative reviews (social media and review websites) if they are unhappy with their experience with a business.
- If a business can build a reputation for high quality, it can develop a competitive advantage.
- Good quality can be achieved through quality control or quality assurance.

The Difference between Quality Control and Quality Assurance

Quality Control

- **Quality control** is where finished products are inspected to see if they meet minimum standards.
- This approach checks for product defects rather than preventing defects from occurring.
- Quality standards are achieved before products reach customers; if a product is found to have a defect it is rectified or sold as a sub-standard product.
- This approach is costly as it could result in a large amount of wastage because the end of the production process is too late to test for quality, and quality is checked by inspectors and not by workers.

Quality Assurance

- **Quality assurance** is where quality is part of the production process; quality is checked at every stage by workers.
- Every worker takes responsibility for quality; although time consuming, this approach should result in zero defect production.
- Workers are more motivated as they are involved in decision making.

- Quality inspectors are not required but management must train workers effectively and set up adequate systems to test quality and reduce inconsistencies.
- Customers' needs are prioritised in the production process and businesses can assure customers that products are good quality.

The Importance of Managing Quality

- If a business has effective quality management systems, they experience less wastage in defective products and the cost of production is lowered.
- If the cost of production is lower, profit margins increase.
- Good quality products meet customer expectations; happy customers make repeat purchases and recommend goods and services to friends and family, which leads to further word-of-mouth sales.
- Building quality management into the production process can be expensive. A business will weigh this up against the potential increased sales from customers and brand reputation for good quality.
- A business will need to invest the time in finding out customer expectations as they differ based on the business, e.g. customers have different expectations from a budget airline and a premium airline.
- To gain a competitive advantage, a business needs to offer better quality goods or services than competitors at a competitive price.

Budget airline

Premium airline

Quick Test

1. Which quality management method involves quality inspectors performing quality tests once a product has been made?
2. How can businesses assure customers that products are good quality when using the quality assurance approach?
3. How do efficient quality processes help a business to gain a competitive advantage?

Key Words

quality
quality control
quality assurance

The Sales Process

You must be able to:

- Discuss the factors that contribute to an effective sales process
- Analyse the importance to a business of providing good customer service.

The Sales Process

- In the sales process, **product knowledge** is important for a sales person as it enables the features and benefits of products to be effectively communicated to customers.
- Sales people should have the ability to match a customer's needs to suitable products on offer by the business; the customer can then make an informed choice.

- **Speed and efficiency of service** are fundamental to ensuring customer needs are met; customers should be served in a timely manner and be provided with the correct items that have been requested.
- Customers may have different standards, dependent on the nature of the business, e.g. a fast food restaurant is expected to serve customers quickly, but in a restaurant a longer wait is expected.
- Customer engagement is concerned with the experiences of customers with a business or brand and the connection that is built through nurturing and managing this relationship.
- Customer engagement can be achieved through various channels of correspondence, both offline and online.
- If a business can keep customers engaged, their interest can turn into sales.

- A response to customer feedback is required to maintain good relationships with customers.
- A business needs to ensure that positive and negative **customer feedback** is acted on as this is effective market research.
- If a customer is unhappy with a business or leaves a bad review, this must be handled in a sensitive way to try and resolve the situation and to keep the customer's business.
- Post-sales service is concerned with the procedures that a business has in place to support customers after the sale of a good or service. Examples include warranty or repair services.

Customer Service

Good Customer Service

- Good customer service has many benefits for a business.
- Happy customers feel valued, are loyal and will repeat purchase.
- If customers are loyal to a business, it is much harder for competitors to get them to try their products.
- Satisfied customers tell others about their good experiences and this could attract more people to the business.
- Satisfied customers can help create a positive working environment and make a business a reputable employer.
- A business can gain a reputation for good customer service and this can develop into a competitive advantage.

Bad Customer Service

- Poor customer service will lead to complaints and a loss of sales for a business.
- Bad customer service can have a negative impact on the reputation of a business as customers may share their negative experiences with family and friends or post bad reviews online for new potential customers to see.
- Bad reviews can have a negative impact on overall sales for a business, lowering revenue and profit.
- A loss of reputation can contribute to a business losing its position in the market, or can leave it vulnerable to being taken over by competitors.

> **Quick Test**
>
> 1. What are the **five** factors that are important in the sales process?
> 2. Name **one** benefit of offering good customer service.
> 3. How can poor customer service impact a business?

> **Key Words**
>
> sales process
> customer engagement
> post-sales service

1 What is meant by function? [1]

The capability of a product and it's function.

2 Why will a business use an extension strategy? [1]

So they can change the product so people want it/more sales.

3 Why may a business decide to reduce the price of a product during the decline stage? [2]

A business may reduce the price so they can get rid of it.

4 What is a freemium? [2]

A pricing strategy used for online games as the game is free but people pay for advantages

5 State the **five** promotion strategies. [5]

Special offers
branding ~~advertising~~
sponserships
product trials
advertising

6 What is sponsorship? [2]

Sponsorships are when businesses give a brand money, in return they advertise the business.

7 How can a business use targeted advertising online in promotion? [2]

Cookies help track what people are intrested in So they know who to adverties to.

8 What is a distribution channel? [2]

9 Give **one** example of how retailers add value to products. [1]

10 What is e-commerce? [1]

11 Explain how the price element of the marketing mix influences place for Internet-only businesses. [2]

12 Why do the elements of the marketing mix need to be balanced? [1]

1 State **one** advantage of the job production process. [1]

Workers are motivated as jobs are different.

2 Explain the flow production process. [2]

Large numbers of products are created at once.

3 How has technology increased the productivity of businesses? [2]

Technology has increased production as the machines can work 24/7 so more can be created.

4 What are the **three** types of stock? [3]

~~Thosminatione~~ raw matirials

Finished goods

Stocks of matirials

5 What is minimum stock level (buffer stock)? [1]

The lowest amount a business will hold

6 Why are supplier relationships important if a business operates just in time stock control? [3]

It's important as they require regular deliveries so stock can be ordered with short noties and arrive in good time and quality.

7 What is meant by quality? [2]

Quality is how good a product is and the matirials used.

8 Which method of managing quality may result in a large amount of wastage? [1]

Just in time stock

9 Why is it important for workers to receive effective training if a business uses the quality assurance approach? [3]

10 How can a business use the sales process to collect market research? [2]

11 What is post-sales service? [2]

It's where they offer customer support after the product has been deliverd.

12 How might customers respond if they receive bad customer service? [1]

They may tell people and not recomend it.

Business Calculations

You must be able to:

- Understand the concept and calculation of gross profit and net profit
- Calculate and interpret gross profit margin, net profit margin and average rate of return.

Sales Revenue

- **Sales revenue** is:
  - how much a business receives in payment from selling goods and services
  - also called 'income', 'revenue' or 'turnover'.
- A business needs to know how much revenue it has received to be able to calculate profit (once costs are deducted).
- The formula for sales revenue is: selling price × quantity sold.

Costs

- **Costs** are the operating expenses a business must pay.
- A business needs to know how much its costs are to be able to calculate profit (after deducting costs from sales revenue).
- Different types of costs: **fixed costs**, **variable costs** and **total costs**.

Fixed costs
• Stay the same regardless of output • Are **indirect costs** (not directly linked with the production of the goods or service being produced and sold) • Remain the same regardless of how many goods or services are made and sold • E.g. rent, advertising, manager salaries

Variable costs
• Change directly with the level of output • Are usually **direct costs**, which are directly linked with the production of goods or services • The more goods or services made and sold, the higher variable costs will be • Are also known as **cost of goods sold** • E.g. raw materials, raw ingredients, wages of temporary staff

Total costs
• Are calculated by adding all fixed costs and variable costs together

What is Profit?

- **Profit** is the difference between how much revenue a business receives and how much it has to pay out in costs.
- Profit is difficult to make in the first year or two of operation; so a **loss** is often made by new businesses.
- **Gross profit** is the calculation of how much profit a business

makes from selling goods or services after it has deducted the cost of sales (costs incurred directly).
  – The formula for gross profit is: sales revenue – cost of sales.
  – Gross profit should be expressed in units of currency, e.g. £.
- **Net profit** is found after other operating expenses are deducted (such as fixed costs) and bank interest.
  – The formula for net profit is: gross profit – other operating expenses and interest.
  – Net profit should be expressed in units of currency, e.g. £.

Profit/Profitability

- Profit and profitability are not the same thing.
- Profit is how much profit has been made.
- Profitability looks at how good a business is at making a profit.

Profitability Ratios

Profitability ratios help a business:
- calculate its ability to make profit
- measure how effectively the business converts revenues into profit
- measure whether the profit is enough to finance reinvestment
- measure how well the business compares with the rest of the industry it operates in.
- **Gross profit margin** is: gross profit/sales revenue × 100. The answer should be expressed as a percentage (%).
- Gross profit margin shows how efficient a business is in converting the cost of sales bought into profit.
- The lower the gross profit margin, the more stock a business has to sell to make a sustainable profit.
- **Net profit margin** is: net profit/sales revenue × 100.
- When this formula is used, the answer is expressed as a percentage (%).
- Net profit margin shows how profitable a business is when all costs are taken into account.
- If the net profit margin is considerably lower than the gross profit margin, it suggests that overheads are high and should be reduced.
- The **average rate of return (ARR)** is: average annual profit (total profit/no. of years)/cost of investment × 100.
- When this formula is used, the answer should be expressed as a percentage (%).
- ARR calculates how much an entrepreneur or investor is getting back on the money invested and can be compared to bank interest rates.
- ARR does not take cash-flow into account.

> **Key Point**
>
> Gross profit looks at how much profit a business has made on the revenue they have received once the cost of sales has been deducted. Net profit looks at how much profit has been made after all costs have been deducted.

> **Key Words**
>
> sales revenue
> costs
> fixed costs
> variable costs
> total costs
> indirect costs
> direct costs
> cost of goods sold
> profit
> loss
> gross profit
> net profit
> profitability
> gross profit margin
> net profit margin
> average rate of return (ARR)

> **Quick Test**
>
> 1. Explain the difference between gross profit and net profit.
> 2. Explain the difference between profit and profitability.
> 3. Explain what average rate of return is.

Understanding Business Performance

You must be able to:

- Use and interpret quantitative business data to support, inform and justify business decisions
- Understand the use and limitations of financial information in business performance and decision making.

What is Quantitative Business Data?

- Quantitative business data is numerical and statistical data.
- Businesses use graphs and charts to present a lot of quantitative data in one place.
- Graphs, tables and charts are a visual and easy way of expressing information and can often show trends and other important considerations.
- Sometimes businesses share quantitative data in the form of numbers, such as percentages, which show accuracy and allow for comparisons with historic figures, other businesses and the industry standard.
- Quantitative business data can be collected from primary or secondary sources:
  - primary data is collected first-hand by someone for a specific reason
  - secondary data relates to information that is second-hand.

Key Point

Quantitative data is useful, however it needs to be accurate and interpreted correctly to be of proper use, especially if it is being used to base business decisions on.

What is Financial Data?

- Financial data refers to past, present and future records of the financial health of a business, e.g. financial and accounting records, sales, marketing and salary data.
- Sharing of some financial data is mandatory, while some can remain private.
- Sole traders and partnerships have to share financial records of their income, expenses, VAT records (if they are over the VAT threshold) and Pay As You Earn (PAYE) records (if they hire staff).
- Sole traders have to keep bank statements as proof. However, this data is not shared with the public.
- Companies have to provide copies of their accounts every year and file them with Companies House; these accounts include balance sheets and statements of profit and loss, which are available for the public to view.
- Unlike sole traders and partnerships, companies must also pay auditors to prepare their accounts for them.

How can Financial Data be Used?

- Financial data can be used to:
  - show trends within a business
  - apply to a bank for a loan
  - apply to investors for investment analysis.

What is Marketing Data?

- **Marketing data** is data that helps a business make decisions.
- It may be data that a business has collected themselves (primary data), e.g. from a questionnaire about customer preferences, or it could be data that already exists (secondary data), which the business finds useful.
- Marketing data has information about sales forecasts, promotional plans and customer preferences.

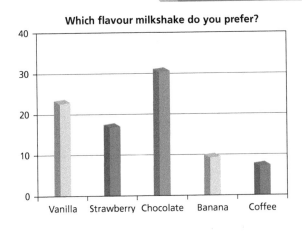

Which flavour milkshake do you prefer?

What is Market Data?

- **Market data** refers to information that relates to a variety of investment markets, including:
  - live prices of stocks and shares on the stock exchange market
  - exchange rates on the currency markets that show the latest buying and selling rates for different currencies
  - **commodities** on the commodity market that show the price of many of life's necessities, which can affect everyone, e.g. oil.

The Use and Limitations of Financial Information

- Many stakeholders use financial information to interpret past business performance.
- This can show if a business has been successful.
- Limitations of financial information include:
  - it may only be a snapshot of a certain period of time
  - it can quickly become out of date
  - it may be inaccurate as the data collected may be biased or might have missed out vital contributing factors
  - two people reading the same quantitative data may have different ways of understanding it.

Key Words

quantitative business data
financial data
marketing data
market data
commodities

1. Which production process takes a long time and requires highly skilled workers? [1]

2. Explain the batch production process. [2]

3. Which production process would be most suitable for a business that wants to make identical products in large quantities? [1]

4. How does a reliable supplier help a business to gain customer satisfaction? [3]

5. What is meant by the term 'procurement'? [2]

6. Name **three** costs associated with holding large quantities of stock. [3]

7. Which method of managing quality involves checking for quality during the production process? [1]

8 Explain why effective quality management systems lead to a more motivated workforce. [3]

....

....

....

9 Explain how a reputation for good quality products can benefit a business. [3]

....

....

....

....

10 What is customer engagement? [2]

....

....

11 Why is product knowledge important in the sales process? [1]

....

....

12 How does customer service lead to repeat purchases for a business? [3]

....

....

....

1. What is sales revenue and why is it relevant? [3]

Revenu is ~~revenue~~ relevant as its the profit the business

2. What are fixed costs? [2]

Fixed costs are costs that don't change like rent.

3. What are variable costs? [2]

Variable costs are costs that change like raw matirials this could also be wages as they are paid by the hour

4. Complete the following table to calculate the net profit for a business. [4]

Sales revenue (£)	Fixed costs (£)	Variable costs (£)	Net profit/loss (£)
650	150	600	-100
1050	500	300	+250
380 000	150 000	200 000	+30000
4 000 000	90 000	1 000 000	~~+4910000~~ +2910000

5. Castle Bouncers are a firm who hire out bouncy castles for parties. Their monthly fixed costs are £150 per month and the variable costs for each party hire is £50 in petrol and labour. Castle Bouncers charge £100 to hire the castles for each party. They aim to make nine party bookings each week. Calculate the net profit or loss Castle Bouncers will make each week if they meet their aim. Show your workings and the formula used. [3]

450+ 37.5 = 487.5

9×100= 900

6 What is the formula for gross profit margin? [1]

gross profit ÷ sales revenu ×100

7 Consider the following two projects and calculate the average rate of return (ARR) for both, then suggest the best project to invest in. [6]

	Project One (£)	Project Two (£)
Capital investment	(50 000)	(70 000)
Year 1 annual profit	20 000	20 000
Year 2 annual profit	30 000	50 000
Year 3 annual profit	40 000	50 000

90000 ÷ 3 = 30000 / 50,000 ×100 = 60%.

120000 ÷ 3 = 40,000 / 70,000 ×100 = 57%.

The best project to pick is project 1 as you get more reter return so they get more.

8 What is quantitative business data? [1]

Satistical data

9 Name **one** type of account that a company must file with Companies House. [1]

Organisational Structures

You must be able to:

- Explain different organisational structures and when each are appropriate
- Explain the importance of effective communication
- Assess different ways of working.

Organisational Structures

- **Organisational structures** are:
- charts that look similar to family trees – they can be **hierarchical** (also known as tall) or **flat**.
- useful to show the internal structure and the roles and responsibilities of staff in businesses.

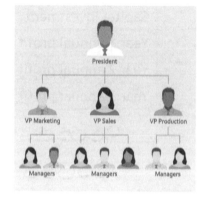

Hierarchical Structures

- Have lots of levels of authority.
- Can motivate staff to strive for the next level of promotion due to their many management levels.
- Can be expensive (lots of managerial salaries).
- Communication can be slow and distorted due to numerous levels of authority.
- Examples: NHS, local government, the police force.

Flat Structures

- Have few levels of authority.
- Are responsive to change (staff have the **autonomy** (authority) to make decisions).
- May leave staff feeling overwhelmed if few levels of management for support.
- Examples: small family businesses, the creative industries.

Business Decisions

- Some businesses prefer big decisions to be made by senior management in a head office; this is known as being **centralised**.
- With centralisation all branches or stores of a business will have the same policies, prices and look.
- Centralisation can slow communication between the shopfloor and senior management – to overcome this, some businesses prefer to be **decentralised**.
- Decentralised businesses make decisions at a local level, by local managers who know what their customers' needs are and can quickly respond to them without having to refer to Head Office.

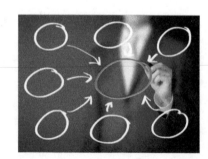

Effective Communication

- It is vital for a business to have strong communication with all of its managers, staff and customers; this minimises mistakes.
- A business with too little communication can leave staff feeling ignored and stressed; without specific communication, staff may make wrong decisions, causing mistakes, wastage, loss of time and poor motivation levels.
- A business with too much communication can give staff too much information; staff might feel overwhelmed by emails or by attending too many meetings.
- Sometimes communication is poor due to other reasons, such as:
  - it uses too much jargon
  - it uses the wrong language, which is open to misinterpretation
  - it may be biased or untruthful
  - it may not seek feedback (or act upon feedback) from staff or customers.

 Key Point

Too much communication is just as risky as too little communication.

Different Ways of Working

- Full-time staff work for around 35 hours per week (and, due to regulation, no more than 48 hours per week).
- Part-time staff gain the same benefits as full-time staff but work for less than 35 hours a week.
- Working hours can be rigid, e.g. 9–5, or flexible.
- Flexible hours are when someone will work the number of hours they are contracted to but with more choice over when they work.
- Contracts may be permanent (on an 'until-further-notice basis') or temporary.
- Businesses may have staff they permanently hire (on a full-time, part-time or flexi-time basis) for day-to-day work and recruit temporary staff for busy periods or to cover staff holiday or sickness (on a temporary basis).
- Freelance contracts are when someone is self-employed and they choose to work for different businesses on a contract-by-contract basis.
- Freelance workers tend to be highly specialist, e.g. architects.
- Technology has brought change to the work environment; people are able to work together from different locations, which is known as remote working.

Key Words

organisational structure
hierarchical
flat
autonomy
centralised
decentralised
motivation
jargon
full-time
part-time
flexible hours
permanent contracts
temporary contracts
freelance contracts
remote working

Quick Test

1. Explain what an organisational structure is.
2. Explain the difference between a centralised and a decentralised structure.
3. Explain the term 'remote working'.

Effective Recruitment

You must be able to:

- Explain different job roles and responsibilities
- Explain how businesses recruit people and the documents required to do this.

Key Job Roles

- Sole traders and partnerships are the main decision makers for their business, however they may want or need to employ staff to work with them.
- Private limited companies and public limited companies have boards of **directors** who are the people responsible for the business. Directors:
  - meet regularly to decide the aims and objectives of the business
  - make decisions that affect all the stakeholders, not just the company's shareholders
  - are the people who decide whether dividends will be paid (paying profits to shareholders)
  - need to be aware of their legal responsibilities as directors
  - may decide to employ **senior managers** to be responsible for the day-to-day operations of the business in order for aims and objectives to be achieved.
- Senior managers might need to hire **supervisors** or **team leaders** to help them communicate with, manage and motivate staff.
- Supervisors and team leaders work with staff and have the authority to delegate work, reward and discipline staff; as **line managers**, they are in charge of staff during their shift and are normally paid a higher salary for this responsibility.
- **Operational staff** are staff hired to look after other day-to-day jobs, such as receptionists and administration staff.
- **Support staff** are those who carry out specific jobs that facilitate business success, e.g. (IT) technicians, canteen staff.

Internal Recruitment

- **Internal recruitment** is when a business appoints someone for a job who already works for the business.
  With internal recruitment:
  - the member of staff is familiar with the business and the business knows the applicant is reliable
  - there is no need for expensive advertising and induction training
  - if a member of staff moves from one role to another within the business, their old job still needs to be filled

- some members of staff may be resentful if a colleague is promoted for a job they desire
- methods of advertising include: notices in staff rooms, emails, management recommendation and announcements at meetings.

External Recruitment

- **External recruitment** is when a business hires people from outside of the business.
  With external recruitment:
  - new recruits are often highly motivated and productive
  - new recruits will require expensive induction training, time to settle into the role; they may also need support from other staff, which might slow existing staff productivity
  - advertising for external recruitment can be an expensive and lengthy process, e.g. senior members of staff might have to **give notice** of three months with their existing employer
  - methods of advertising include: online advertising, notices in Job Centres, recruitment agencies, advertising in newspapers.

Documentation for Recruitment

- A **CV** (curriculum vitae) is a summary of personal, career, education and skills details.
- An applicant may leave their CV with a business to consider.
- A **job description** is a document prepared by a business that explains the responsibilities and duties of a job.
- A **person specification** is a document prepared by a business that explains what they are seeking in any applicant for a job; it lists essential and desirable qualifications, skills, attitudes, characteristics and experience.
- A **job application form** is a form prepared by a business for a candidate to complete when applying for a job. An application form allows specific questions to be asked, in a format that helps a business to treat all staff equally.

Hiring process

Job Posting > Review of Applications > In-Person Interview > Job Testing > Job Offer

Quick Test

1. Explain what hierarchy is and give some job examples.
2. Assess how useful external recruitment is.
3. State the **four** main documents required for the recruitment process.

Effective Training and Development

You must be able to:

- Explain how businesses train and develop employees
- Explain why businesses train and develop employees.

What is Training and Development?

- **Training** is the action of teaching a person new skills.
- **Development** is improving or perfecting existing skills.

Types of Training

Formal Training

- **Formal training** is when a business arranges for staff to have training that has specific objectives. Formal training:

  - is provided by specialists and tends to be away from work, e.g. when employees go on a course to gain a new qualification with other learners from different businesses
  - is highly structured; upon completion the employee may be given a certificate
  - is of a high standard; it allows employees to learn without interruptions
  - is expensive and takes a member of staff away from the workplace.

Informal Training

- **Informal training** is when a business arranges for staff to receive less structured training. Informal training:

  - usually takes place within the workplace and involves other team members to provide training
  - is useful for teaching staff how to use specific equipment, e.g. how to use a till
  - can be tailored to the employee in a familiar setting
  - is quick and cheap to arrange
  - is sometimes not taken seriously and relies on the expertise of the trainer.

Self-learning

- **Self-learning** is when an employee studies without the presence of a teacher or colleague. Self-learning:
  - often includes computer courses, online learning and watching videos
  - allows employees to learn at their own pace
  - is cheap
  - does not allow the learner to get immediate feedback or questions answered because there is no teacher.

Observation

- Observation (often called 'shadowing') is when an employee watches another member of staff to learn how a job is done. With observation:
  - staff are able to ask questions
  - the member of staff being observed is able to check understanding by asking questions
  - sometimes members of staff do not enjoy being observed, which can cause resentment
  - the training is only as good as the member of staff being observed; they may teach bad habits.

Training and Business Target Setting

- Successful businesses tend to regularly review their aims and objectives.
- This involves constantly reviewing legal, marketing, customer needs and technological changes; this can help with target setting.
- Staff need to be trained to keep up with all of these changes through ongoing training.
- Through regular appraisals with staff, businesses can identify gaps in knowledge or skills and devise a training plan by setting targets for individuals, monitoring their progress through performance reviews.
- Performance reviews are formal and give staff feedback on their performance over a period of time.

Why Businesses Train and Develop Staff

- Businesses need to train staff to be able to carry out their roles effectively.
  Staff who are better trained:
  - are more likely to produce better quality goods and services, which means less wastage and more efficiency, which reduces costs
  - can be more productive, which can benefit the business and help them produce more
  - have higher levels of motivation and are more likely to enjoy their roles, giving better customer service
  - attract new recruits to the business who are interested in career development.

> **Key Point**
>
> Training and developing staff can be expensive but if done effectively can help staff keep up to date with changes in technology, bringing business efficiency and competitiveness. Staff training and development also improves productivity, quality and staff motivation.

> **Key Words**
>
> training
> development
> formal training
> informal training
> self-learning
> observation
> ongoing training
> appraisals
> performance reviews

> **Quick Test**
>
> 1. Explain what formal training is.
> 2. Explain what self-learning is.
> 3. Explain why an employee might be more motivated if they are trained.

Motivation

You must be able to:

- Explain the importance of motivation in the workplace
- Explain how businesses motivate employees.

A Motivated Workforce is Good for Business

- Motivation is about encouraging staff to want to give their best effort and care about the business they work for.
  A motivated workforce:

  - is more likely to attract new recruits because if applicants see that people are enjoying their work, they are more likely to want to work for the business; the more applicants a business has, the larger a talent pool they have to choose from, which means they should be able to hire the best quality staff
  - is more likely to recommend others to come and work for their firm, which can save on job advertising costs
  - can reduce staff turnover, which is the percentage of staff who leave a business during a certain period of time
  - is more likely to bring new ideas to a business because they care about its success

  - is more likely to give better customer service because their satisfaction shows
  - is more likely to be productive and efficient, which can increase quality output and reduce mistakes, thus increasing profit.

Financial Methods of Motivation

- Remuneration means financial payment for work completed or services performed.
- Some people are motivated by high remuneration and work harder if they know they will be paid more.
- Workers on a piece rate (which is a method of paying staff according to how many pieces of work they produce) may be motivated to work more quickly to produce more goods or services if they know their wages will be higher, however a business will need to make sure that quality does not suffer if workers rush their jobs.

- Some businesses pay staff a bonus if they reach certain targets.
- Bonuses can be an incentive for staff to try their hardest to achieve a relatively hard target, which is a motivator for people who like a challenge.

- However, businesses have to be careful their staff do not cut corners to reach these targets. Also, after the target is reached, some staff stop giving their best effort because they have already been rewarded.
- **Commission** is a method used to pay staff once they have either made or sold something.
- With commission, the employee tends not to receive any payment until they have made or sold something particular, e.g. an estate agent will be paid once a house has been sold.
- **Fringe benefits** (perks) are when a business rewards its staff with something of financial value, such as free gym membership.
- Fringe benefits are not always taxed, or are taxed at a lower rate, so the employee benefits from a higher net income.
- Some staff are interested in fringe benefits because they can save them a lot of money in expensive life luxuries.
- **Promotion** is another financial motivator; if staff know there is possibility of promotion to a higher level of work, they may be more likely to perform to their best ability.

Non-financial Methods of Motivation

- **Job enrichment** is when a business tries to make a job more demanding and less boring in order to motivate staff.
- Some low skilled, boring jobs can benefit from **job rotation**, which means that staff are given short periods of time on various jobs before they move onto other jobs.
- Praising staff is sometimes the most effective method of motivation.
- **Autonomy** involves giving staff responsibility to manage their own work; this allows staff to feel trusted, which can be motivating.

Key Point

A business can provide financial rewards or non-financial rewards to motivate staff.

Key Words

staff turnover
remuneration
piece rate
wages
bonus
commission
fringe benefits
promotion
job enrichment
job rotation

Quick Test

1. Explain what the term 'motivation' means.
2. Explain **one** benefit to a business of having a motivated workforce.
3. Explain what a fringe benefit is.

1   What are costs, and why are they relevant? [2]

....

....

2   What are indirect costs? [1]

....

3   What does the term 'cost of goods sold' mean? [2]

....

....

4   Complete the following table to calculate gross profit for a business. [4]

Sales revenue (£)	Cost of goods sold (£)	Gross profit (£)
380	150	
2500	300	
150 000	45 000	
6 000 000	170 000	

5   Nice Ice make ice lollies and sell them for £2 each. The fixed costs Nice Ice have to pay each month are £3000 and the variable costs are 60p per ice lolly. Calculate Nice Ice's net profit/loss if they sell 1400 ice lollies in one month. Show your workings and the formula used. [3]

....

....

....

6   Explain why a business would want to use profitability ratios. [5]

....

....

....

....

7 Business One makes £750 000 revenue with £250 000 left as gross profit, and Business Two makes £500 000 revenue with £350 000 left as gross profit. Calculate the gross profit margin for both businesses and identify the business that is most profitable. [5]

8 Consider the following two projects and calculate the average rate of return (ARR) for each, then suggest the best project to invest in. [8]

	Project Pink (£)	Project Blue (£)
Capital investment	(500 000)	(1 200 000)
Year 1 annual profit	50 000	500 000
Year 2 annual profit	250 000	600 000
Year 3 annual profit	900 000	700 000

1. What is a disadvantage of a flat organisation? [1]

2. What does the term 'decentralised' mean? [2]

3. Give an example of poor communication within a business. [1]

4. Who makes the main strategic decisions for private limited companies and public limited companies? [1]

5. Assess the value of a business choosing internal recruitment. [8]

6 Explain the difference between a job description and a person specification. [2]

7 What is the difference between training and development? [2]

8 What is self-learning? Give an example. [2]

9 Explain **one** benefit of a motivated workforce. [3]

10 What are fringe benefits? Give an example. [2]

1 What are 'tall' organisations? [1]

2 What is **one** advantage of a business running with a centralised organisation? [1]

3 What are freelance workers? [1]

4 Can sole traders employ staff? [1]

5 Assess the value of external recruitment. [8]

6 Name **one** disadvantage of formal training. [1]

7 Explain how training by observation could be useful. [3]

_____

_____

_____

_____

8 What does the term 'remuneration' mean? [1]

_____

9 What does the term 'job enrichment' mean? [1]

_____

_____

10 What does the term 'empowerment' mean? [1]

_____

_____

11 Explain how regular staff appraisals can help a business with training and business target setting. [3]

_____

_____

_____

12 Explain what piece rate remuneration is and explain **one** disadvantage of this form of work. [3]

_____

_____

_____

_____

Mixed Questions

Answer these questions on a separate piece of paper.

1. Provide **two** examples of primary research a business might conduct. [2]

2. A business has fixed costs of £10000. The selling price for their product is £10 and their variable cost per unit is £5.
   Calculate the break-even point. [3]

3. What does the term 'just in time' mean? [1]

4. What are the **six** stages of the product life cycle? [6]

5. Is survival a more appropriate objective for a new business rather than an established business?
   Justify your answer. [3]

6. Explain what happens to customer spending when interest rates increase. [3]

7. Do sole traders have limited or unlimited liability? [1]

8. What are the benefits of share capital over taking out a loan? [3]

9. Give **two** examples of a cash outflow. [2]

10. Calculate the profit using the information below. [6]

    Selling price = £10

    Sales quantity = £100

    Fixed cost = £20

    Variable cost per unit = £5

11. What is the difference between a job description and a person specification? [2]

12. Outline **one** strategy a bakery might use to get a customer to trial a product. [2]

13. How might globalisation benefit a customer? [3]

14. What are the benefits of using retained profit as a source of finance? [4]

15. Why do governments charge tax on employees' income and business profits? [2]

16 What is the difference between limited and unlimited liability? [2]

17 What is the formula for total profit? [1]

18 What is the difference between qualitative and quantitative data? [2]

19 State **three** financial objectives of a business. [3]

20 Provide a disadvantage of having low buffer stock levels. [3]

21 Provide **three** features of a public limited company. [3]

22 Outline **one** benefit of taking out a loan over using share capital. [2]

23 Is break even measured using pounds or quantity (units) sold? [1]

24 What does the term 'market map' mean? [1]

25 Identify **three** non-financial methods to motivate workers. [3]

26 Explain **one** benefit of using written communication. [3]

27 What is the difference between quality control and quality assurance? [2]

28 Would using mass advertisement be useful for businesses targeting niche markets? [3]

29 Explain the impact of increased globalisation on a UK business. [3]

30 Why might two businesses manufacturing cars merge with each other? [3]

31 What is the purpose of employment law? [3]

32 Outline **one** reason why it is important that a business has cash. [2]

33 What is the formula for revenue? [1]

34 What is the definition of a business? [1]

35 What does the term 'commission' mean? [1]

Mixed Questions

36 Out of job, batch and flow production, which method would you use to make a suit for world-famous footballer David Beckham?
Justify your answer. [3]

37 Explain the impact on the level of imports if sterling appreciates in value. [3]

38 Explain how social media might increase the sales of a business. [3]

39 Give **two** limitations of a partnership. [4]

40 Can you provide **two** examples of secondary research a business might conduct? [2]

41 Describe the role of an entrepreneur. [2]

42 Explain **one** way a business can improve productivity. [3]

43 Why might a business use a centralised approach? [3]

44 Outline **one** benefit of quality assurance. [3]

45 How might target advertising online increase the sales of a business? [3]

46 How does the Internet allow a business to be more competitive internationally? [3]

47 What does the term 'takeover' mean? [1]

48 What possible conflicts might there be between a customer and a shareholder? [3]

49 Outline **one** benefit of venture capital. [2]

50 Give an example of two businesses whose objectives are likely to differ.
Explain why they are different. [3]

51 What is the formula for gross profit margin? [1]

52 What is the purpose of a tariff? [2]

53 What does the term 'inflation' mean? [1]

54 Explain **one** way e-commerce can reduce the costs of a business. [3]

55 Calculate the closing balance on the following cash-flow forecast.   [2]

> Inflow: £5000
>
> Outflow: £3000
>
> Opening balance: £5000

56 What is the difference between a fixed cost and a variable cost?   [2]

57 Give **three** examples of customer needs when entering a clothes shop.   [3]

58 List **two** ways a new business idea may come about.   [2]

59 Why is it important for a business to provide ongoing training to its employees?   [3]

60 What is the difference between a flat and a hierarchical organisational structure?   [2]

61 State **three** factors you may want to consider when choosing a supplier.   [3]

62 Why is it important for a business to differentiate their products?   [3]

63 Why might a business's objectives change over time?   [3]

64 How might the economic climate affect a hotel business?   [3]

65 List **three** things that might go into a business plan.   [3]

66 What does the term 'insolvent' mean?   [1]

67 How might income affect a business's decision on who to target?   [3]

68 What is the formula to calculate profit?   [1]

69 What is the difference between a shareholder and a stakeholder?   [2]

70 List the **three** elements of the design mix.   [3]

71 Give **one** example of a trading bloc.   [1]

72 How might employment be affected in a recession?   [2]

Mixed Questions

73 List **three** examples of a stakeholder. [3]

74 Give **two** examples of short-term finance for a business. [2]

75 Explain why it might be important for businesses to retain their employees. [3]

76 State **one** document that would be used in the recruitment process. [1]

77 Explain why a business might hire freelance workers rather than permanent workers. [3]

78 Explain what might be an issue to a bakery of having high maximum stock levels. [3]

79 Explain the possible trade off between ethics and profit. [3]

80 Explain why a UK business might move its production to a developing country. [3]

81 How might increased legislation affect a business? [3]

82 Outline the purpose of a business plan. [2]

83 What is the formula for total cost? [1]

84 Give **two** variables you might see on a market map. [2]

Answers

Pages 6–7
1. Adapt goods and services to meet customer needs.
2. Changes in technology; Changes in consumer tastes; Goods and services becoming outdated.
3. An adaptation of a good or service that is already on the market.

Pages 8–9
1. Business failure; Loss of money; Lack of a secure income.
2. Careful planning and market research.
3. The owner having independence and making his/her own business decisions.

Pages 10–11
1. Goods.
2. To provide goods and services to meet consumers' needs, while making a profit.
3. Capital; Land; Labour; Enterprise.

1. To survive **[1]** and grow **[1]** and continue to meet the changing needs of customers **[1]**.
2. A business will be first to meet customer needs for that good or service **[1]** and can benefit from high profits **[1]**.
3. C **[1]**
4. The demand for goods and services can change **[1]**. A business needs to adapt to meet these changing preferences and to remain current **[1]**.
5. The things that may go wrong when setting up a business **[1]**.
6. Being in full control as the boss **[1]**, making all the business decisions **[1]** and deciding when and what times to work **[1]**.
7. Not having financial security as entrepreneurs give up employment **[1]** and do not have a guaranteed regular income **[1]**. There is a risk that financial commitments cannot be met if the business isn't successful **[1]**.
8. C **[1]**
9. To provide goods or services to meet customer needs **[1]**.
10. An entrepreneur will need to have the required characteristics and skills to run a business **[1]**. This involves taking risks, being creative and the ability to make important decisions **[1]**. Enterprise is needed to organise the other factors of production to start a business **[1]**.
11. Branding **[1]**; Quality **[1]**; Convenience **[1]**; Design **[1]**; Unique selling point **[1]**.
12. Branding creates a well-known image for the good/service **[1]**, making the business stand out from competitors **[1]**. Customers are willing to pay a higher price for a branded good/service **[1]**.

Page 14–15
1. **Any three from**: price, quality, choice, convenience, service.
2. To satisfy the different wants of customers. Customers have different preferences.
3. If the customer believed that British Airways provides a better quality service than easyJet.
4. If customers' needs are met they will purchase from the business, providing more revenue and potentially more profit for the business. They become loyal customers and repeat purchase. They spread good news about the business to family and friends and provide good reviews.

Pages 16–17
1. Market research is a process of collecting information about what consumers want, market trends and competitors.
2. Primary research; Secondary research.
3. Quantitative data.

Pages 18–19
1. Market segmentation involves breaking down a market into smaller groups (segments).
2. **Any three from**: location, demographics, lifestyle, income, age.
3. Two features.
4. Gap in the market and competitors.

Pages 20–21
1. A competitive environment is a market where there are many businesses selling similar goods and services.
2. **Any one of**: lower profits, businesses can find themselves in a price war, consumers may think the good or service is poor quality.
3. Businesses need to focus on differentiating their goods or service to gain a competitive advantage. Businesses need to decide how they can meet customers' needs better than competitors.

1. A **[1]**
2. A business can set up and start selling online immediately **[1]**. New goods and services have come about and the business can now expand its customer base **[1]**. Businesses can use social media to communicate with and advertise to their customers **[1]**.
3. A business that is always changing to meet customer needs **[1]**.
4. Make products that better meet the needs of customers **[1]**, create new versions of old products **[1]** or add additional features **[1]**.
5. Having a successful business **[1]**, making a profit **[1]** and having independence **[1]**.
6. They have unlimited liability **[1]**, which means owners can lose personal possessions if the business runs up debts **[1]**.
7. Business sales **[1]** or profit over time **[1]** and market share **[1]**.
8. Conduct market research **[1]** and undertake careful planning to find out what customers want **[1]**.
9. A good is a physical product, e.g. a car **[1]**, whereas a service is not a physical object, e.g. dentistry provided by a dentist **[1]**.
10. A characteristic or feature that makes a product unique **[1]**.
11. Adding value increases the worth of a product **[1]**. A business must do this to cover the cost of producing goods/services **[1]** and to ensure that it can make a profit **[1]**.
12. A unique feature or design will make a good or service stand out from its competition **[1]** and attract customers **[1]** who will be willing to pay a higher price **[1]**.

1. The needs and wants of customers when purchasing a product **[1]**.
2. Customers have different tastes and preferences **[1]**.
3. Through identifying customer needs the business can meet them **[1]**. This is likely to generate sales **[1]** and ensure the survival of the business **[1]**.
4. **Any three from**: survey **[1]**, questionnaire **[1]**, focus group **[1]**, observation **[1]**.
5. They have a limited amount of money **[1]** and some market research methods are expensive **[1]**.
6. Online reviews or comments about goods and services can determine what a customer thinks about a business's product or that of a competitor **[1]**. Online focus groups and surveys can be used to collect data quickly and cheaply **[1]**. Hashtags can be used to track trends **[1]**.
7. Quantitative data is numerical and can be measured easily **[1]**. Qualitative data is opinions, judgements and feelings and cannot be put into a numerical form **[1]**.
8. **Any four from**: location **[1]**, demographics **[1]**, lifestyle **[1]**, income **[1]**, age **[1]**.
9. Customers are grouped by how they live their life **[1]** and the choices that they make **[1]**.
10. Competitors **[1]**, the position of products within a market **[1]**, gaps in the market **[1]**.
11. Businesses need to focus their decisions on how they can make their products different from competitors **[1]** to gain a competitive advantage **[1]** and to meet the needs of customers more precisely than the competition **[1]**.
12. Provide goods and services that better meet the needs of customers **[1]**.

Pages 26–27

1. An aim explains what the long-term goal of a business is. An objective is a short-term step the business will take in order to achieve its overall aim.
2. To allow the business to share its direction with staff so they know what to focus on and are motivated to perform; to enable a business to measure its performance and to help a business plan for the future.
3. Financial aims and objectives typically relate to money, e.g. profits. Non-financial aims and objectives relate to goals that are not money-related, e.g. personal challenge.

Pages 28–29

1. Fixed costs are costs that remain the same regardless of the level of output. Variable costs relate directly to the level of output and vary accordingly.
2. Contribution means how much each unit made and sold contributes towards the fixed costs or profit of a business.
3. The formula for break even is: fixed costs/contribution per unit. At break even no loss or profit has been made.

Pages 30–31

1. A cash-flow forecast helps identify the timing of when, in the future, cash is paid into and out of a business.
2. All businesses need to be able to pay bills or expenses on time to avoid becoming insolvent.
3. Cash is money coming into a business or money held in a bank account. Profit is: revenue – total costs.
4. Negotiating with suppliers for longer credit terms; Sending invoices to customers as soon as they place an order; Selling unwanted assets.

Pages 32–33

1. Short-term finance must be repaid within one year, whereas long-term finance can be repaid over a longer period of time.
2. The advantage of trade credit is that a business can receive payment from its own customers *before* it pays the suppliers, removing the need for the business to raise its own finance.
3. Overdrafts offer convenience, speed and flexibility, with interest charged only on the amount of money borrowed. Loans are lump sums provided to a business by a bank over the medium- to long-term, which are repaid by the business to the bank via equal monthly repayments.

1. Price [1]; Quality [1]; Convenience [1]; Service [1]; Choice [1].
2. A successful business must understand what its customers want in advance in order to be competitive [1]. Keeping up to date with changes in fashion and taste is also important as customer needs continually change [1].
3. Customers want the best quality for the most reasonable price [1].

4. **Any three from**: more sales and revenue [1], leading to more profit [1], good customer reviews [1], repeat purchase/ loyal customers [1].
5. Identify if there is enough demand to make the business successful [1].
6. Primary research involves collecting new information specific to the needs of a business [1]. Secondary market research uses data that already exists [1].
7. Interviews [1] or focus groups [1] in which open-ended questions can be asked to gain in-depth answers.
8. Breaking down the market into smaller groups (segments) [1], which contain people with similar wants, needs or characteristics [1].
9. To identify where a product will be placed in a market [1] compared to other similar products in the same market [1].
10. A gap in the market may have been identified because there is no demand for it [1].
11. To find ways to make their goods and services different from the competition [1].
12. **Any one of**: buying cheaper raw materials to make cost savings [1], offering exceptional customer service [1], providing excellent quality [1] and offering promotions and loyalty discounts [1].

1. **Any two from**: to allow the business to share its direction with staff [1], motivating staff to perform [1], to enable a business to measure its performance [1], to help a business plan for the future [1].
2. **Possible answer**: A privately owned restaurant may aim to survive its first year of trading [1], whilst a charity may aim to raise as much money as possible for a cause [1]. The main difference is profit is either kept with the private owner, or given away as charity [1].
3. **Any three from**: survival [1], profit [1], volume of sales [1], market share [1], financial security [1].
4. Business costs that change directly [1] with the level of output goods or services [1].
5. Fixed costs + variable costs [1]
6. £10 per unit – £6 per unit is a contribution of £4 per unit [1].
7. Break even is where total costs = total revenue [1]. At this point, a business is not making any loss or any profit [1].
8.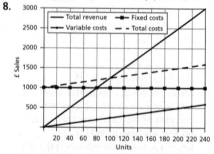

The break even is 100 units [1]. Margin of safety is 240 units – 100 units = 140 units [1].

9. **Any two from**: cash paid out of a business to pay suppliers [1], wages [1], loan repayments [1], advertising costs [1] and overheads [1].
10. Total revenue – total costs [1]
11. When external investors (venture capitalists) with a lot of business experience are willing to invest considerable funds into a business at their own risk [1], however in return venture capitalists often demand a high share of profits [1] and shared control of the business [1].
12. Selling assets can raise finance for a business that needs cash and has unwanted assets to sell [1], which means more cash can be brought into the business [1] to be available to pay bills on time [1].

Pages 38–39

1. A sole trader; A partnership.
2. **Any three from**: owner can lose personal belongings, hard to raise finance, owner can lose money if sick, owner can lose money if on holiday, high amount of tax if profit is high.
3. An arrangement between an established business (the franchisor) that allows other businesses or individuals (franchisees) the right to sell goods and services using its name, trademark and business processes.

Pages 40–41

1. Nature of the business; Market; Labour; Materials; Competitors.
2. Customers will already shop in the location and the business can be another choice for customers if they decide to shop around.
3. Easy to set up a new business without the need for premises. A business can outsource manufacturing to cheaper locations. An online marketplace means that a business doesn't need to be located close to customers.

Pages 42–43

1. Promotion.
2. A business will need to balance their marketing mix and identify (depending on their market) which element of the marketing mix is the most important for them to focus on.
3. The Internet gives customers access to information, making them more knowledgeable about prices, so some businesses have to change their prices to remain competitive. A business may be able to lower its prices due to cost savings made thanks to technology.

Pages 44–45

1. The business idea, business aims and objectives, target market, forecast revenue, cost and profit, cash-flow forecast and sources of finance.
2. Helps to see if the business has potential to be a success so that the money borrowed can be paid back with interest.
3. Having a plan helps the owner think about all aspects of the business; to set clear aims and objectives and to address any areas that need attention.

1. Often for new businesses costs are very high and revenue is relatively low [1], which means that the business needs to be able to pay bills on time in order to stay solvent [1]. Established businesses tend to have objectives which are profit or market-share related [1].
2. Society [1] or the environment [1].
3. **Any three from**: salaries [1], rent [1], advertising [1], fixed loan repayments [1].
4. When costs [1] are higher than revenue [1].
5. When a business does not have enough cash [1] to pay its bills [1].
6. Overdraft [1]; Trade credit [1].
7.
   Selling price = £10
   Sales quantity = 100
   Fixed cost = £20
   Variable cost per unit = £5

   Revenue – total costs = profit [1]
   Revenue = selling price £10 × 100 = £1000 [1]
   Variable costs = £5 × 100 = £500 [1]
   Total costs = £500 variable costs + £20 fixed costs [1]
   Profit = £1000 – £520 = £480 [1]
8. Break-even formula for level of output is: fixed costs/selling price – variable cost per unit [1].
   Break-even formula for level of output is: fixed costs/selling price – variable costs × selling price.
   Break even level of output is:
   £20/£10 – 5 = 4 units [1] × £10 = £40 level of sales [1].
9. **Any three from**, benefits: quick to obtain [1], easy to obtain [1], does not incur any interest [1]; drawbacks: a business in its first year of trading will not have have any retained profit [1], once retained profit is used, there is less retained profit to use for other needs or emergencies [1].
10. By taking a bank loan, a business would not need to share profit with the bank [1]; whereas raising finance via share capital would mean having to pay increased dividends to shareholders [1].

1. A franchisee pays the franchisor a fee [1] in exchange for using their name, their products and their business process [1].
2. A sole trader (business owner) and his/her business are seen as one entity [1]. The owner has unlimited lability [1] and is at risk of losing personal possessions if the business incurs debts [1].
3. **Any one of**: more capital can be raised by partner [1], partners bring a range of skills [1], problems and decisions are shared [1].
4. Nature of the business [1]; Market [1]; Labour [1]; Materials [1]; Competitors [1].
5. Businesses need to be where the raw materials are located [1].
6. Businesses need to be near suitably skilled staff [1] who are willing to work for the wages that are being offered [1].
7. Product [1]; Place [1]; Price [1]; Promotion [1].
8. Place is about how businesses get products to customers when and where they are willing to buy them [1]. This

can be via business premises [1], the Internet [1] or through a retailer [1].
9. Businesses can use the internet to sell their products [1] and target customers anywhere in the world [1]. Money can be saved by not needing physical business premises [1].
10. To help raise money from banks and other lenders [1].
11. **Any three from**: the business idea [1], business aims and objectives [1], target market [1], forecast revenue [1], cost and profit [1], cash-flow forecast [1], sources of finance [1], location [1], marketing mix [1].
12. Makes entrepreneurs look at all aspects of the business and address all areas [1]. Costly mistakes can be avoided as the business is well planned out [1] with clear aims and objectives [1].

Pages 50–51
1. A stakeholder is any person who has an interest in a business and is affected by the activities of a business.
2. Customers seek quality for a fair price; Suppliers seek businesses able to pay bills on time; Banks want to provide bank accounts and lending facilities to successful businesses.
3. When different stakeholders have conflicting wants from a business, e.g. staff want high wages but shareholders want high profits.

Pages 52–53
1. The activity of buying and selling goods and services online.
2. Technology has helped to reduce manufacturing costs, which means businesses can reduce their selling prices.
3. Product: more technology now in many products; Price: reduced costs have helped reduce selling prices; Place: customers can buy online; Promotion: use of social media and online marketing.

Pages 54–55
1. A strict set of legal rules within which businesses operate.
2. Discrimination; Minimum wage.
3. Goods and services must be fit for purpose; As described; Of satisfactory quality.

Pages 56–57
1. The broad performance of a country's economy, measured by GDP.
2. When workers have less money to spend, they also tend to buy cheaper products, and fewer products.
3. Consumers with borrowing will have to pay more interest to banks, which means they have less money to spend.

Pages 58–59
1. Emails, video calls and websites to search for and carry out employment make it easier and quicker to communicate.
2. The Trading Standards Authority checks that businesses adhere to strict rules when selling goods and services; this protects the public from being sold counterfeit goods.
3. Inflation is when the average price level increases.

1. **Any one of**: expensive to set up [1], other franchisees could damage their brand image [1], continued payment to the franchisor [1], cannot make own decisions [1].
2. The legal responsibility for an owner to pay the debts of a business [1].
3. The ownership type will determine the liability [1]. An owner is at risk of losing personal possessions if the business they start has unlimited liability [1].
4. This gives business the opportunity to be an alternative choice if customers decide to shop around [1].
5. Some businesses do not need a physical location and can set up an online business [1].
6. Some small businesses do not need a physical location [1] and can set up and run online [1].
7. If prices are too high [1], customers may choose to buy cheaper alternatives [1].
8. Customers' needs change all the time [1] and a business will need to adapt their marketing mix [1] to keep up with customer needs [1].
9. New promotions opportunities [1], e.g. using email or social media. This is cheaper than some other promotion methods, saving the business money [1].
10. A document that summarises the future objectives of the business and shows how they will be achieved [1].
11. A cash-flow forecast shows forecasted monthly cash inflows and outflows [1], allowing an entrepreneur to see when money may need to be borrowed to cover negative cash-flow [1].
12. The business plan includes the legal responsibilities of the business and these can be researched [1] so that they can be adhered to and planned for [1].

1. Managers [1]; Employees [1]; Owners [1].
2. Supplying the business with goods of excellent quality [1], which customers will want to repeat purchase [1]. However, if supplies are of poor, or even dangerous quality, customers may choose to buy goods elsewhere in the future [1].
3. Shareholders tend to expect high dividends from the business [1]. Employees want to receive the highest wages they can [1].
4. **Any three from**: ability to compare prices of suppliers [1], removing need for physical premises [1], removing need for many staff [1], improved technology [1].
5. When a business treats all job applicants and workers fairly [1] regardless of, **any three from**: gender [1], age [1], race [1], religion [1], disability [1], sexual preference [1], type of contract [1], stage of pregnancy [1].
6. When a business examines all work areas to reduce the chances that an employee will come to harm [1].
7. The goods or services must be able to do what they were designed to do [1].

8. The amount of money consumers have left to spend after they have paid their taxes and living expenses [1].
9. Businesses that focus on selling cheaper products [1].
10. A tax that is added on top of selling prices for goods and services bought from any business [1], which is then passed to the government [1].
11. The cost (to the business)/price (to the consumer) of exchanging one currency for another [1].
12. To protect the buying rights of the public when purchasing goods and services [1]. The Act explains what consumers can expect when buying goods and services and what their refund rights are [1].
13. The Trading Standards Authority checks that businesses adhere to strict rules when selling goods and services to protect the public from being sold counterfeits [1]. It also makes sure that the weights and measures of business products are accurate so consumers are sold the exact quantities they are expecting and have paid for [1].

Pages 64–71 Revise Questions

Pages 64–65
1. Organic growth is when a business grows on its own. Inorganic growth is when a business merges with (or takes over) another business.
2. It is cheaper, because no interest is charged, and the finance is available more quickly.
3. It has to be repaid and is costly (due to interest being charged).

Pages 66–67
1. To change their aims and objectives as the business evolves to adapt to changing circumstances.
2. It may need to enter new markets, exit old markets or change its product range.

Pages 68–69
1. When organisations and businesses trade internationally.
2. Imports are when products made overseas are brought into the UK. Exports are when a business makes products in the UK then sells them to other countries.
3. A tariff is a tax that is added onto the selling price of an imported good, making it more expensive for importers to import into a country.

Pages 70–71
1. Ethics are moral guidelines for good behaviour.
2. The majority of businesses operate to make profit. In order to make profit businesses need to produce goods and services cheaply, which might mean non-ethical behaviour such as paying wages that are below the legal requirement.
3. Businesses that act in a non-ethical way may suffer public criticism and a drop in sales as a result of this criticism.

Pages 72–73 Review Questions

1. People who have an interest in a business who are outside of the business [1]. **Any one of**: customers [1], suppliers [1], banks [1], any other suitable answer [1].
2. By providing excellent customer service [1], which helps to boost the reputation of the business [1]. On the other hand, staff with poor customer service can drive away customers [1].
3. **Any two from**: local investment [1], jobs (employment) [1], limiting pollution (business takes responsibility towards the environment) [1].
4. Technology has encouraged innovation [1] and has introduced new products to replace obsolete ones [1].
5. Being exploited by businesses [1] who want to pay workers wages that are too low to live on [1].
6. **Any three from**: not to be discriminated against [1], to earn a minimum wage [1], not to work excessive hours [1], time off work to care for dependants [1], the right to work in a safe environment [1], to be treated fairly if made redundant [1].
7. To avoid being heavily fined and/or having staff sent to prison [1], which would impose financial penalties on the business [1], which could cause the failure of the business [1]. Also to maintain a good reputation with the public and its customers [1] so they continue to shop with the business or recommend the business [1] and therefore improve revenue for the business [1].
8. Lower levels of spending [1] and/or buying products that are cheaper [1].
9. 625 bears × $8 each = $5000 [1] $5000/1.25 = £4000 [1]
10. Bob could either buy more bears for the same amount of money [1], or he could benefit from lower costs for the 625 bears he is buying [1].
11. **Any eight from**: businesses that borrow money from banks with loans that do not have fixed interest rates will find that their interest repayments increase [1], which means a rise in costs [1], which they may either decide to absorb or pass on to customers, if they are willing to pay extra [1]. Consumers will also find their borrowing costs will increase (e.g. credit cards/mortgage) [1], which will reduce their disposable income [1], leading to less cash to spend [1], which means they are likely to buy less from businesses, or change to buying inferior products [1]. This will lead to businesses having to either reduce their prices to match the willingness and ability of customers to pay lower prices [1] or they may need to consider offering inferior products that customers are attracted to [1]. The decision of the business will depend on the price sensitivity of consumers [1].

Pages 74–75 Practice Questions

1. The more products a business makes and provides, the cheaper it is to make each product [1] because the unit cost for each will reduce [1].
2. Inorganic growth can bring faster growth [1], benefit a business from shared resources and capital [1] and bring new ready-made customers [1].
3. Members of the public are invited to buy shares in the company [1].
4. Aims are the long-term goals of a business [1]; objectives are the short-term steps a business takes to realise those goals [1].
5. If a business has not met its aims and objectives, it will need to revisit them to see if they were realistic and may need to make amendments for the future [1].
6. When work is sent overseas to a host country [1], which is any country that welcomes the operation of foreign businesses [1].
7. When restrictions are put in place to make it difficult for other countries to trade [1].
8. When certain countries group together [1] to agree to make it easier for them to market goods, services, capital, and labour [1] by getting rid of all barriers to trade [1].
9. **Any one of**: pay a fair wage to workers [1], ensure production does not harm the environment [1], ensure production does not harm animals [1], ensure production does not harm people [1].
10. The long-term use of resources and suppliers [1], which does not lead to environmental damage [1].
11. By promoting its ethics as an added value [1], which promotes a good reputation for the business [1], which appeals to customers who wish to buy ethically [1].
12. Merger [1]; Takeover [1].
13. There may not be any retained profit in the business, especially if the business is new [1], the funds might be needed for something else [1], once the money has gone it is not available for future unforeseen problems [1].

Pages 76–85 Revise Questions

Pages 76–77
1. Function; Aesthetics (appearance); Cost.
2. Making changes to the product (re-branding, lower price) or appealing to a new market segment.
3. **Any three from**: brand image, unique selling point, offering a better location, features, function, design, and appearance, cheaper selling price, quality, customer service, product range.

Pages 78–79
1. **Any one of**: a low starting price that is increased later, a price to reflect the brand and quality of the product, high margin–lower volume or low margin–higher volume, high starting price that is reduced later or setting prices in line with competitors.
2. New pricing strategy – freemium. Digital products are offered for free with a premium for additional features,

functionality or virtual goods. More discounts and comparison websites so prices need to be competitive. Better machinery and tools mean manufacturing is quicker, which saves costs and increases profit.

3. During introduction, the price helps to determine the value of a product, push sales or recover development and promotion costs. During the decline stage, a reduced price is a final try at achieving as many sales as possible.

Pages 80–81
1. Younger generations regularly use social media so advertising can be based on popular social media websites; more interactivity makes advertising more appealing to younger generations.
2. Buy one, get one free can be used for mass market products as they are sold in high volumes.
3. **Any one of**: targeted advertising online, viral advertising via social media, e-newsletters.

Pages 82–83
1. It is important to get products available in the right place at the right time, so that customers can make their purchase.
2. A retailer has a physical location to sell their goods and services. An e-tailer sells their goods and services via the Internet.
3. They buy products from manufacturers at one price and add their own mark-up, so that customers pay more.
4. Customers can shop at any time from any location and have products delivered to them without the need to physically visit a shop.
5. Customers want their orders delivered quickly.

Pages 84–85
1. False.
2. The price of a product helps to determine which promotion methods are used. A high-priced, high-quality product will be promoted differently to a product that has a low price. For example, it is unlikely that Mercedes will use a buy-one, get-one-free offer to promote their luxury cars. Instead, they may prefer to pay for a car magazine article highlighting its features, which would appeal to its target market.
3. By making their product innovative.

Pages 86–87 **Review Questions**
1. Increased brand recognition [1], more customers [1], increased revenue and profit [1].
2. When two separate businesses join together [1] to make one new bigger business [1].
3. Share capital is a method for a business to raise funds [1]. A Ltd company can offer family and friends shares in the business in exchange for money [1]. The business will not have to pay back the money or any interest [1], however it will need to share profits with these shareholders [1].
4. If consumers change their taste, a business has to find out what their new tastes are [1] so it can amend its

aims and objectives to ensure customer needs are met [1].
5. **Any one of**: increase its market share [1], increase sales volume [1], increase its brand recognition [1] increase the size of its workforce [1] extend the number of outlets it has [1] increase profit levels [1].
6. **Any three from**: to make the most of British skilled labour and flexible workforce [1], to benefit from being closer to their British and European customers [1], to avoid having to convert currencies [1] to bypass UK import restrictions [1].
7. To stop cheap imports flooding the country [1], making it hard for UK producers to compete on price [1].
8. Adaptation of products to suit local tastes [1]; Price amendments to take currencies and foreign wages into account [1]; Transportation arrangements to place products in other countries [1]; Different promotional techniques to attract foreign customers [1].
9. Poor wages [1]; Working environment lacking health and safety precautions [1].
10. The business could suffer from bad publicity [1], causing customers to boycott it [1], which would lead to a drop in revenue and profit [1].
11. By raising awareness through letter writing to MPs and media [1], staging marches and publicity stunts [1].

Pages 88–89 **Practice Questions**
1. The look, taste or feel of a product are its aesthetics [1].
2. Sales are at their peak [1], further sales growth will be slow as other businesses join the market [1]. Profit may be high [1].
3. **Any one of**: set prices in line with competitors [1], high-price during introduction to give the impression of a premium product [1], low profit margin–high volume [1], or high profit margin–low volume [1].
4. **Any one of**: prices need to be competitive [1] since customers can compare businesses using comparison websites [1]. Businesses have access to better machinery and tools [1], production time is lowered and services can be provided quickly – saving costs and increasing profits [1]. Freemium pricing allows businesses to offer digital products for free [1] and additional features or functionality have to be paid for [1].
5. Customer must be able to afford the products [1], if the price is set too high, products may not sell [1].
6. Strategy identifies how a business gets the right message to its market segment at the right time and in the right way [1].
7. **Any two from**: website advertising [1], social media [1], e-mail adverts [1], banner adverts [1], pop-ups [1], apps [1].
8. Customers need to be able to purchase products at a time they want in a place they want [1].
9. **Any one of**: more interactive [1], captivating [1], links in the e-newsletter can direct customers to where businesses want them to go [1].

10. **Any one of**: it is expensive to set up e-tailing websites [1] and customers may be reluctant to pay for items over the Internet due to fraud [1].
11. An advantage held by a business that allows it to perform better than its rivals [1].
12. If customers demand a low-priced product [1] a business will need to produce it cheaply, reducing their costs and enabling a low price [1] and this will result in a low-quality product [1].

Pages 90–97 **Revise Questions**
Pages 90–91
1. To create goods and services.
2. Job production; Batch production; Flow production.
3. Lower costs; Increased productivity; Improved quality; Further flexibility.

Pages 92–93
1. Maximum stock level; Minimum stock level (buffer stock); Re-order level; Lead time; Order quantity.
2. Just in time stock control is where businesses do not hold any stock. Raw materials and components are ordered in exactly when they are needed and are used straight away in the production process.
3. Quality; Delivery; Availability; Cost; Trust.

Pages 94–95
1. Quality control.
2. Customer needs are a priority; quality is checked at every stage so goods or services should have zero defects.
3. By offering better quality goods and services than competitors at competitive prices.

Pages 96–97
1. Product knowledge; Efficiency of service; Customer engagement; Customer feedback; Post-sales service.
2. **Any one of**: loyal customers that repeat purchase, hard for competitors to take customers, good reviews, more sales, a positive working environment, good reputation and brand, a competitive advantage.
3. Customer complaints, a loss of sales, negative reviews leading to a bad reputation for the business, lower sales, revenue and profit.

Pages 98–99 **Review Questions**
1. The capabilities of a product to perform its intended purpose [1].
2. To prevent a product going into decline [1].
3. Sales are reducing during the decline stage [1], so a lower price may attract customers [1].
4. A pricing strategy usually used for digital products, games or software [1]. Products are offered for free and then a premium is charged for extra features and functionality [1].
5. Advertising [1]; Sponsorship [1]; Product trials [1]; Special offers [1]; Branding [1].
6. A business financially supporting or giving goods or services to an event or

programme [1] in return for advertising their brand [1].

7. Browsing habits of customers can be collected through Internet cookies [1], businesses can then target their promotion based on what customers usually look at online [1].

8. The route that a product takes [1], from where it is manufactured, to where it is sold [1].

9. **Any one of**: free parking [1], product warranty [1], customer service [1].

10. Electronic transactions through the Internet or via an electronic payment system [1].

11. Internet-only businesses can charge a lower price [1] because they don't have to pay the costs associated with premises [1].

12. All four elements influence each other; a successful marketing mix will use a combination of all four elements [1].

Pages 100–101 **Practice Questions**

1. **Any one of**: products are high quality [1], unique and tailored to meet customer needs [1], workers are motivated and take pride in their work [1], and business can charge a high price [1].

2. An automated process [1] where a large number of identical products are made on an assembly line [1].

3. Machines and robots work autonomously [1], unlike workers who need breaks, holidays and time off [1].

4. Raw materials [1]; Stock of materials that are not yet completed (work in progress) [1]; Finished goods [1].

5. The lowest amount of stock that a business wishes to hold at any one time [1].

6. Supplier relations will need to be strong [1], this ensures stock can be ordered with short notice [1] yet arrive in good time and be of good quality [1].

7. Meeting a minimum set of standards [1] to satisfy customer expectations for a good or service [1].

8. Quality control [1].

9. Workers need to know how to effectively check products are meeting the minimum standards [1]. All workers need to have the same standards [1] to ensure there are no inconsistencies in the quality checking process [1].

10. From customer feedback [1], both positive and negative feedback can tell a business how customers feel about its products [1].

11. Procedures that a business has in place [1] to support customers after the sale of a good or service [1].

12. Leave bad reviews of the business [1].

Pages 102–105 **Revise Questions**

Pages 102–103

1. Gross profit is revenue – cost of sales sold. Net profit is gross profit – operating costs.

2. Profitability looks at how good a business is at making a profit. Profit is how much profit the business has made.

3. Average rate of return: total profit/no. of years/cost of investment × 100.

Average rate of return calculates how much an entrepreneur or investor is getting back annually on the money she/he invested.

Pages 104–105

1. Numerical and statistical data.

2. Marketing data is data a business collects to help make decisions. Market data refers to information that relates to a variety of investment markets.

3. Financial information can quickly become out of date, be inaccurate, biased, open to misinterpretation.

Pages 106–107 **Review Questions**

1. Job production [1].

2. Similar items are grouped and made together (in batches) [1]. A new batch is started once one batch has been made [1].

3. Flow production [1].

4. A reliable supplier ensures orders are delivered on time allowing businesses to meet demand [1] and produce good quality products for their customers [1]. This ensures customer satisfaction [1].

5. The act of obtaining or buying raw materials, components or services from a supplier [1] to be used in the production of goods and services [1].

6. **Any three from**: costs involved in storage space [1], insurance [1], employing staff to manage storage [1], interest on borrowing used to buy stock [1].

7. Quality assurance [1].

8. Every worker is responsible for quality [1], which involves workers in decision making [1], thereby increasing motivation [1].

9. Good quality products meet customer expectations [1]. Happy customers make repeat purchases and recommend goods and services to friends and family [1], which then leads to further word-of-mouth sales [1].

10. The experiences of customers with a business or brand [1] and the connection that is built through nurturing and managing this relationship [1].

11. Product knowledge enables a sales person to effectively communicate features and benefits of products to customers [1].

12. Customers will feel valued by the business [1], which creates loyalty [1] and repeat purchases [1].

Pages 108–109 **Practice Questions**

1. Sales revenue is how much a business receives in payment from selling goods and services to customers [1]. The formula for sales revenue is: price × quantity [1]. Sales revenue is relevant because a business needs to know how much revenue it has received in order to be able to calculate profit [1].

2. Fixed costs stay the same regardless of the level of output [1]. Examples of fixed costs are, **any one of**: rent, advertising, manager salaries.

3. Variable costs are costs that change directly with the level of output [1]. Examples of variable costs are, **any one of**: raw materials, raw ingredients, wages of temporary staff.

4.

Sales revenue (£)	Fixed costs (£)	Variable costs (£)	Net profit/loss (£)
650	150	600	100 loss [1]
1050	500	300	250 profit [1]
380 000	150 000	200 000	30 000 profit [1]
4 000 000	90 000	1 000 000	2 910 000 [1]

5. The formula for net profit is: gross profit – other operating expenses and interest [1].
Therefore (9 × £100 = £900 revenue) – (9 × £50 = £450 cost of sales) = £450 gross profit [1].
So, £450 – fixed costs of £150 = £300 net profit [1].

6. Gross profit/sales revenue × 100 [1].

7. Average Rate of Return (ARR) formula is: average annual profit (total profit/no. of years)/cost of investment × 100 [1].
Project One: (£20 000 + £30 000 + £40 000) – £50 000 = £40 000/3 years = £13 333 average profit per year [1].
£13 333/original investment of £50 000 × 100 = 27% (rounded up from 26.66%) [1].
Project Two: (£20 000 + £50 000+ £50 000) – £70 000 = £50 000/3 years = £16 667 average profit per year (rounded up from £16 666.666) [1].
£16 667/original investment of £70 000 × 100 = 24% (rounded up from 23.81%) [1].
Therefore, Project One has the higher ARR and is the better investment [1].

8. Quantitative business data is numerical and statistical data [1].

9. **Any one of**: balance sheets [1], statements of profit and loss [1].

Pages 110–117 **Revise Questions**

Pages 110–111

1. An organisational structure is the internal structure of a business and the roles and responsibilities of the staff who work for it, shown in levels of authority.

2. A centralised structure is where big decisions are made by senior management in a head office. In decentralised structures business decisions are made at a local level by local management.

3. People working away from the business, whether from home or even in different countries.

Pages 112–113

1. Hierarchy is the organisational structure of a business that allows everyone to see who is responsible for what role. Senior management sits at the top of the hierarchy. Middle management, team leaders and supervisors are in the middle of the hierarchy. Workers are at the bottom of the hierarchy.

2. It can bring new talent and fresh ideas to a business, however it can be expensive, time consuming and external staff may need training.

3. CV; Job description; Person specification; Job application form.

Pages 114–115

1. When a business arranges for staff to have training that has specific objectives.
2. When an employee studies without the presence of a teacher or colleague.
3. Staff are more likely to feel appreciated, enjoy their roles and give better customer service.

Pages 116–117

1. When staff want to give their best effort and care about the business they work for.
2. **Any one of**: reduce staff turnover, reduce staff absences.
3. The perks of a business, such as the use of a company car or free gym membership.

1. Costs are operating expenses a business must pay [1]. Costs are relevant because a business needs to know how much its costs are in order to be able to calculate profit [1].
2. Costs that are not directly linked with the production of the goods or service being produced and sold [1].
3. The cost of the raw materials/ ingredients [1] and direct labour needed [1] to create a product.
4.

Sales revenue (£)	Cost of goods sold (£)	Gross profit (£)
380	150	230 profit [1]
2500	300	2200 profit [1]
150000	45000	105000 profit [1]
6000000	170000	5830000 profit [1]

5. Formula is: revenue – total costs = profit [1], therefore, revenue is 1400 × £2 = £2800; total costs are (1400 × 0.60) + £3000 = £3840 [1]; therefore, loss is £2800 – £3840 = -£1040 [1].
6. Profitability ratios can help a business calculate the ability of a business to make profit [1] and what those trends are [1]. They also measure how effective a business is in converting revenues into profit [1], whether the profit is enough to finance reinvestment [1], and how well a business compares with the rest of the industry [1].
7. Gross profit margin formula is: gross profit/sales revenue × 100 as a percentage [1], therefore Business One's gross profit margin is £250000/£750000 × 100 = 33% [1] and Business Two's gross profit margin is £350/£500000 × 100 = 70% [1]. Therefore, Business Two has the higher gross profit margin, which makes it the most profitable business [1] because it has the highest gross profit margin percentage out of the two businesses [1].
8. The Average Rate of Return (ARR) formula is: average annual profit (total profit/no. of years)/cost of investment × 100 [1]. Project Pink: average annual profit is (£50000 + £250000 + £900000) – £500000 = £700000/3 years, is £233333 average profit per year [1]. £233333/£500000 initial investment × 100 = 47% ARR (rounded up from 46.66%) [1].
Project Blue: (£500000 + £600000 + £700000) – £1200000 = £600000/3 years is £200000 average profit per year [1]. £200000/£1200000 original investment × 100 = 50% [1]/3 = 400000 [1]. Therefore, 400000/500000 × 100 = 17% ARR (rounded up from 16.66%) [1]. Therefore, Project Pink has the highest ARR and is the better investment [1].

1. Some staff may be demotivated and feel overwhelmed by their workloads if there are few levels of management to support them [1].
2. When decisions are made at a local level [1] by managers closer to customers [1].
3. **Any one of**: confusing information [1], too much communication [1], too little communication [1], jargon [1], biased communication [1], untruthful information [1].
4. The board of directors [1].
5. Internal recruitment is when a business decides to appoint someone to a job who already works for the business [1]. Positives: There is already a relationship established [1]; The member of staff is familiar with the business [1]; The business knows the applicant is reliable [1]; There is no need for expensive advertising and induction training [1]. Negatives: However, their old job will still need to be filled [1]; Some members of staff may be resentful [1], which could lead to poor teamwork [1].
6. A job description explains the responsibilities and duties of a job and the day-to-day tasks related to the job [1]. A person specification lists the essential and desirable qualifications, skills, attitudes, characteristics and experience an applicant must possess in order to do the job [1].
7. Training is the action of teaching a person new skills [1]. Development is improving or perfecting existing skills [1].
8. When an employee studies without the presence of a teacher or colleague [1]. Then **any one of**: computer courses [1], online learning [1], watching appropriate videos [1].
9. Staff will want to give their best effort [1]. Then **any one of**: attract new recruits [1], workforce are more likely to recommend to other workers [1], lower staff turnover [1], to bring new ideas [1], give better customer service [1], likely to be more productive [1], reduction in mistakes [1].
10. When a business will reward its staff with something of financial value [1]. Then **any one of**: such as the use of a company car [1], free gym membership [1], free travel [1].

1. Tall organisations have many levels of hierarchy [1].
2. **Any one of**: all branches will have the same policies [1], prices and look [1], giving customers an identical experience [1].
3. When someone is self-employed and they choose to work for different businesses on a contract-by-contract basis [1].
4. Yes [1]
5. External recruitment is when a business hires people from outside of the business [1]. Advantages include: new skills or specialised staff [1], fresh ideas [1], new recruits are often highly motivated and productive [1]. However, new recruits will require expensive induction training [1] and will need time to settle into the role and business culture [1]; they may also need support from other staff [1], which might slow existing staff productivity [1].
6. **Any one of**: it is expensive [1], often takes a member of staff away from the workplace [1], could cause staff shortages [1].
7. Watching how a piece of machinery works or watching a member of staff providing customer service is useful because it shows an employee exactly what they have to learn to do [1]. New staff are able to ask questions [1] and the member of staff conducting the training is able to check understanding by asking questions [1].
8. Financial payment to an employee for work or services provided [1].
9. When a business tries to make a job more demanding and less boring in order to motivate staff [1].
10. Giving staff responsibility to manage their own work [1].
11. Businesses can identify gaps in knowledge [1] and devise a training plan for staff by setting targets [1] and monitoring performance against these targets [1].
12. Piece rate is a method of remuneration that pays staff according to how many pieces of work they produce [1]. Staff may feel under pressure to produce as many pieces as they can in order to earn more money [1], which means they may rush their work [1], which may lead to poor quality products.

1. **Any two from**: questionnaire [1], survey [1], interview [1], observation [1], focus group [1].
2. break-even point = fixed cost/ contribution per unit [1]
contribution per unit = selling price – variable cost per unit
10000/(10 – 5) [1] = 2000 units [1]
(Full marks will be awarded for the correct response even if there is no evidence of workings.)

Helpful Tip
To help avoid calculation errors in quantitative questions you should always write down the relevant formula. From there all you need to do is insert the numbers into the formula.

3. Just in time is the term used when a

business only orders stock when it is required; this avoids holding stock within the company [1].

4. Development [1]; Launch [1]; Growth [1]; Maturity [1]; Saturation [1]; Decline [1].

5. Yes, as a new business does not have an established brand image [1], which means customers may be sceptical about purchasing products for the first time [1] and the business will face greater risks due to their lack of experience [1]. **(1 mark is available for identifying a correct point, with 2 additional marks available for explaining the point.)**

6. Customer spending is likely to decrease [1] as it costs more to borrow money [1], discouraging customers from making purchases which need them to borrow from an institution such as a bank [1]. **(1 mark is available for identifying a correct point, with 2 additional marks available for explaining the benefit.)**

7. Unlimited liability [1].

8. **Any three from:** you do not have to pay any money back [1], no interest [1], shared responsibility for the business [1], new ideas [1]. **(1 mark is available for identifying a correct benefit, with 2 additional marks available for explaining the benefit.)**

9. Possible answers, **any two from:** electricity [1], stock [1], labour [1], dividends [1].

10. Total revenue = selling price × quantity
£10 × 100 = £1000 [1]
Variable cost = variable cost per unit × quantity
£5 × 100 = £500 [1]
Total cost = fixed + variable cost
£20 + £500 = £520 [1]
Profit = total revenue – total cost [1]
£1000 – £520 [1] = £480 [1]
(Full marks will be awarded for the correct response even if there is no evidence of workings.)

11. A job description gives details about the role and the responsibilities of the employee [1]. A person specification states the requirements/skills needed for the job [1].

12. **Possible answer:** By offering a free sample [1]. If the customer enjoys the free sample, they are likely to purchase the product [1]. **(Award 1 mark for identifying a correct point, with 1 additional mark for explaining the point. Any responses that list more than 1 explanation will gain a maximum of 1 mark.)**

13. **Possible answer:** Increased choice in products [1]; Cheaper prices due to a lot of competition [1]; Increase in competition means businesses are likely to lower prices in order to remain/become competitive [1].

14. Do not have to pay the money back [1]; There is no interest to pay [1]; There is no loss of ownership via shares [1]; It is a cheap source of finance [1].

15. To pay for public services [1] such as schools, hospitals and police services [1]. **(1 mark will be awarded for a correct reason, with 1 additional mark for explaining the reason.)**

16. Limited liability is when the owner has a separate legal identity to the business and cannot lose personal possessions if the business fails [1]. Unlimited liability is when a business has the same legal identity as the owner and the owner can lose personal possessions if the business fails [1].

17. total revenue – total cost [1]

18. Qualitative data concerns information in the form of opinions and is not easy to statistically analyse [1]. Quantitative data is in the form of statistics, which can be gained from closed questions, e.g. yes/no responses on a questionnaire [1].

19. **Any three from:** survival [1], profit [1], sales [1], market share [1], financial security [1].

20. If there is a sudden increase in demand, the business will run out of stock [1], which can cause long-term damage to the brand image of the business [1]. This in turn is likely to decrease the future revenue of the business [1].

21. **Any three from:** limited liability [1], owners are called shareholders [1], shares can be bought and sold on the stock exchange [1], accounts have to be made available to the public [1], shared ownership of the business [1], profits given to the shareholders are called dividends.

22. You do not lose your stake in your business [1]. This means that the owner will still be able to have full control of the business [1], which means decision making is likely to be quicker. **Other answers include:** keep more of the profit [1], can gain a large sum of finance from a bank that might not be available from other sources of finance [1]. **(1 mark will be awarded for a correct benefit, with 1 additional mark for explaining the benefit.)**

23. Units [1]

24. A market map is a diagram showing two variables, which is used by a business to find a need in their market that is not being met by existing businesses [1].

25. **Any three from:** job rotation [1], job enrichment [1], autonomy [1], appraisal [1], job enlargement [1].

26. Written communication is documented [1] so if workers forget information they can refer to the written text [1]. This means that information is less likely to get lost due to being recorded, and can be referred to [1]. **(1 mark will be awarded for identifying a correct benefit, with 2 additional marks available for explaining the benefit.)**

27. Quality control is when the standard of the product is checked at the end of the production process [1]. Quality assurance checks the product at every stage of the production process [1].

28. No [1], as mass advertising is expensive [1], and would only be applicable to very specific sets of customers [1].

29. A UK business would face greater competition [1], which would result in a loss in sales, as customers now have more choice [1]. It may also force the UK business to charge cheaper prices so it will take them longer to break even. However, the UK business has a potentially much larger target audience trading internationally so this makes it easier for them to expand [1].

30. **Any three from:** less competition if they merge [1], they can share ideas if they merge [1], brand image can be developed as the business can merge with an already established business within the market [1], technology can be enhanced as one of the businesses merging may have more developed technology available [1], economies of scale are advantageous if the company is bigger as it means it is able to achieve cheaper unit costs with increased output [1].

31. To ensure that businesses do not harm or exploit their employees [1]. This allows the employees to work in a safe environment [1], such as having safety procedures when working on a building site so the employees are not put at risk [1].

32. A business must have cash so that it can pay day-to-day expenses such as labour and materials [1] needed for the business to continue to be able to trade [1].

33. selling price × quantity [1]

34. A business provides tangible goods and intangible services to its customers [1].

35. Commission is when an employee receives payment based on how many sales they make (more sales = more commission) [1].

36. Job production [1], as it allows for higher quality and is personalised to the customer's requirements [1]. A customer such as David Beckham is likely to be less price sensitive and more interested in quality due to his high income and celebrity status [1]. **(1 mark will be awarded for identifying the correct form of production, with 2 marks available for explanation of the form of production.)**

37. Imports are likely to increase [1] as foreign products will become cheaper [1] and customers are less likely to buy British products [1].

38. **Any three from:** many businesses, e.g. Apple, use social media sites to raise awareness of their products [1], social media can reach a wide range of customers [1], with some businesses having millions of followers; increased awareness of the products a business

makes/sells is likely to increase sales [1], promotion by the business through their social media sites [1], word-of-mouth promotion through customer social media sites [1], online-only promotions via social media [1].

39. A limitation of a partnership is that the business has unlimited liability [1]. This means that if the business goes into debt, the owners can lose their personal possessions [1]. Share profit is another limitation as the owners will need to share all profits [1] made by the business equally [1]. **Other possible answer**: Share decision making. **(1 mark will be awared for each limitation identified, with an additional 1 mark for each limitation explained, up to a maximum of 4 marks.)**

40. **Any two from**: Internet [1], already published market reports [1], government reports [1].

41. **Any two from**: an entrepreneur is someone who starts and owns a business and takes risks aiming to exploit a gap in the market [1], they have several roles, including managing resources [1], and making important decisions, such as setting objectives [1].

42. Technology can improve productivity [1], as machinery that is more advanced will be able to produce products at a quicker rate [1]. This means that more products can be produced in the same amount of time [1]. **(1 mark will be awarded for identifying one way of improving productivity, with 2 marks available for explanation.)**

43. A centralised approach allows for decisions to be made quickly [1] as the business owner does not need to consult staff before taking action [1]. Senior management may also have more experience to make better informed decisions [1].

44. A benefit of quality assurance is that quality is everyone's responsibility [1]. This provides an incentive for employees to produce high-quality work [1], which means the finished product is likely to meet customer needs [1]. **Other possible answer:** zero defects [1], less product wastage [1], competitive advantage [1]. **(1 mark will be awarded for identifying a correct benefit, with 2 additional marks for explaining the benefit.)**

45. Advertisements are targeted at customers who have shown an interest in the products [1] and therefore the business is likely to receive a high response rate [1]. This in turn is much more likely to generate increased revenue for the business [1].

46. If a customer has access to the Internet, they will be able to view business information [1]. This allows greater reach for businesses to advertise their products [1] and sell them abroad [1]. **(1 mark will be awarded for identifying one way of being competitive, with 2 marks available for explanation.)**

47. When one business buys out another business [1].

48. A conflict may arise between customers and shareholders as the owners of the business want maximum profits [1]. This means they will charge as high a price as possible [1]. Customers, on the other hand, want the cheapest prices possible so that they can retain as much of their income as possible, causing a conflict [1]. Other possible conflicts: between suppliers and owners; between pressure groups and owners; between employees and managers.

49. A benefit of venture capital is that a business does not need to pay the investor back [1]. Therefore, this is a cheap source of finance that can be provided on a large scale [1]. **(1 mark will be awarded for identifying one correct benefit, with 1 additional mark available for explaining the benefit.)**

50. **Possible answer**: Cancer Research shops and Tesco are two companies with different objectives [1]. Cancer Research shops have a social objective, which is to raise money to fund research into cancer [1], whereas Tesco has a financial objective, which is to make a profit [1].

51. gross profit margin = sales/cost of sales × 100 [1]

52. A tariff is a tax put on buying foreign products by the government to reduce imports [1]. The higher the tariff, the higher the price for customers – this means that customers are encouraged to purchase domestically-produced goods [1].

53. The term inflation refers to the increase in price levels within an economy [1].

54. Not having to pay rent and utility bills at a store [1] will likely reduce the costs of the business, as e-commerce is conducted on the Internet rather than via a physical store [1]. This in turn will allow the business to have lower costs [1].

55. Inflow: £5000
Outflow: £3000
Net cash-flow: £2000 [1]
Opening balance: £5000
Closing balance: £7000 [1]
(Full marks will be awarded for the correct response even if there is no evidence of workings.)

56. A fixed cost is a charge that does not change regardless of how many products a business produces [1]. A variable cost will change with the number of products a business produces [1].

> **Helpful Tip**
> You need to remember that variable costs change with output, while fixed costs will remain the same regardless of how many products are sold.

57. **Any three from**: price [1], quality [1], choice [1], convenience [1].

58. **Any two from**: changes in technology [1], consumer tastes [1], goods and services that are no longer demanded [1].

59. A business must continue to train workers in order to increase productivity [1]. If workers are productive, it means they are able to produce more at the same labour costs [1]. This means the business can charge a cheaper selling price, making them more competitive [1]. Other points to identify and explain could include: motivation; reduced labour turnover. **(1 mark will be awarded for identifying a correct point, with 2 more marks available for explaining the point chosen.)**

60. A flat organisational structure has a short chain of command but a wide span of control [1]. A hierarchical structure has a tall chain of command and a narrow span of control [1].

61. **Any three from**: quality [1], cost [1], speed [1], reliability [1], availability [1], trust [1].

62. If a business differentiates its products it will give them a unique selling point over the competition [1], which is likely to increase the sales of the business [1] as they will have a competitive advantage [1].

63. As a business begins to develop a strong brand image and has an established customer base they may switch from an initial objective of survival to profit [1]. A number of businesses fail in the initial stages of trading so have an objective of surviving [1]. Once the business has been established, it would then look to maximise its profits [1].

64. A high level of unemployment due to a lack of economic activity will result in less demand for holidays [1] so hotels are likely to have less sales [1]. As a holiday staying in a hotel is a want rather than a need it is likely to be something customers will cut back on [1].

65. **Any three from**: business idea [1], business aims and objectives [1], target market [1], sales forecast [1], cash-flow forecast [1], sources of finance [1], marketing mix [1].

66. When a business is no longer able to pay its debts it is insolvent [1].

67. If the business is going to charge a high price for their product they are unlikely to be successful targeting customers on low incomes [1] as they won't be able to afford the transaction [1]. These customers are more likely to be price-sensitive and will base their decision largely on the price [1].

68. profit = total revenue – total cost [1]

69. A shareholder is an owner of a limited company [1]. A stakeholder is anyone that has an interest in the business, such as a customer or an employee [1].

70. Function [1]; Aesthetics [1]; Cost [1].

71. **Any one of**: European Union (EU) [1], North American Free Trade Agreement (NAFTA) [1], Association of South East Asian Nations (ASEAN) [1], any other recognised trade bloc [1].

72. Many businesses are unlikely to have as much demand for their products [1], so

they will not need as many workers, so unemployment will increase **[1]**.

73. **Any three from**: owner **[1]**, supplier **[1]**, customer **[1]**, local community **[1]**, pressure groups **[1]**, government **[1]**.

> **Helpful Tip**
> A common mistake is confusing a shareholder with a stakeholder. A shareholder is an owner of a business, while a stakeholder is any person/organisation that has an interest in the business.

74. **Any two from**: overdraft **[1]**, trade credit **[1]**, factoring **[1]**.

75. Reduced training costs for new staff **[1]**, experience means the workers are likely to be more productive **[1]**. This means they are able to produce more efficiently, reducing the costs for the business and allowing them to offer more competitive prices **[1]**.

76. **Any one of**: application form **[1]**, curriculum vitae **[1]**, job description **[1]**, person specification **[1]**.

77. They will not have to allow the workers paid holiday or pay for any sick days they are absent from work **[1]**. No need for redundancy pay **[1]**. The project may only be a temporary one **[1]**.

78. Food is perishable so stock is likely to be wasted **[1]**, if the business holds too much stock then they have increased their costs **[1]** without increasing their revenue **[1]**.

79. If a business behaves ethically it can result in its costs going up **[1]**, e.g. if it was using cheap labour in a foreign country, it may have to pay those workers more, which will increase costs **[1]**. However, if the business continues to use cheap labour it is likely to damage the reputation of the business and discourage customers from buying their products, resulting in a lack of sales **[1]**.

80. **Any three from**: cheap labour **[1]**, which means cheaper production costs **[1]**, which allows the business to charge lower prices **[1]**, giving them a competitive advantage **[1]**.

81. **Any three from**: following more rules and regulations usually results in increased costs **[1]** to abide by them, e.g. having to employ a new member of staff to enforce/oversee new legislation, this means the costs of the business will rise **[1]**, resulting in having to charge higher prices to customers **[1]**.

82. Mainly to gain finance from a bank **[1]** but also helps the business to make better informed decisions **[1]**.

83. fixed cost + variable cost **[1]**

84. **Any two from**: price **[1]**, quality **[1]**, location **[1]**, customer service **[1]**, product range **[1]**.

Formulae

Total costs
TC (total cost) = TFC (total fixed costs) + TVC (total variable costs)

Revenue
Revenue = price × quantity

Break even
$$\text{Break-even point in units} = \frac{\text{fixed costs}}{(\text{sales price} - \text{variable cost per unit})}$$

Break-even point in costs / revenue = break-even point in units × sales price

Margin of safety
Margin of safety = actual or budgeted sales − break even sales

Interest (on loans)
$$\text{Interest (on loans) in \%} = \frac{\text{total repayment} - \text{borrowed amount}}{\text{borrowed amount}} \times 100$$

Net cash-flow
Net cash-flow = cash inflows − cash outflows in a given period

Opening and closing balances
Opening balance = closing balance of the previous period

Closing balance = opening balance + net cash-flow

Gross profit
Gross profit = sales revenue − cost of sales

Gross profit margin
$$\text{Gross profit margin (\%)} = \frac{\text{gross profit}}{\text{sales revenue}} \times 100$$

Net profit
Net profit = gross profit − other operating expenses and interest

Net profit margin
$$\text{Net profit margin (\%)} = \frac{\text{net profit}}{\text{sales revenue}} \times 100$$

Average rate of return
$$\text{Average rate of return (\%)} = \frac{\text{average annual profit (total profit / no. of years)}}{\text{cost of investment}} \times 100$$

Glossary

Add value: the increased worth that a business creates for a product; it is the difference between what a business pays its suppliers and the price that it is able to charge for the good/service.

Advertising Standards Authority (ASA): a body that ensures all advertising claims are accurate and true so consumers are not misled.

Aims: the long-term goals of an organisation.

Appraisals: when members of staff meet with their line manager to review their work over a period of time.

Assets: something of value to the business, such as machinery or land.

Autonomy: when a member of staff is given freedom to make decisions, they are given autonomy.

Average Rate of Return (ARR): calculates how much an entrepreneur or investor is getting back on the money invested in a business so they know how profitable their investment is.

Bar gate stock graph: a stock control diagram used to determine when new materials should be re-ordered.

Batch production: a production process in which similar components or goods are made together in groups (batches).

Bonus: addition to the basic wage or salary, e.g. for achieving a target.

Boycott: when customers avoid a business because they disapprove of their actions.

Brand: a named product that consumers see as being different from other products and which they can associate and identify with.

Break even: the level of output where total revenues are equal to total costs; this is where neither a profit or loss is being made, i.e. how many units need to be sold to cover all costs but not yet make a profit.

Business location: the place where a business operates.

Business ownership: the different legal structures of a business.

Business plan: a plan for the development of a business, detailing how the business will achieve its goals.

Capital: another name for money.

Cash-flow: the flow of cash into and out of a business.

Cash-flow forecast: making a prediction of the future cash inflows and outflows of a business, usually over the period of a month.

Cash inflow: the flow of cash into a business, e.g. from sales/sale of assets/raising capital.

Cash outflow: the flow of cash out of a business to pay, e.g. salaries, rent, suppliers.

Centralised: businesses with many branches (such as restaurant chains/retail shops) prefer big decisions to be made by senior management in a head office, which all branches then follow.

Click-through rate: the number of people who visit a web page who click on a hypertext link to a further website, usually for sales purposes.

Closing balance: the amount of money a business has in its account at the end of a period of time, e.g. a month, a financial year.

Commission: payment system usually operated for sales staff where their earnings are determined by how much they sell.

Commodities: raw materials such as oil, wheat, metals, coffee.

Companies House: in the UK, the official government organisation that keeps a record of all UK companies and information about them. A company that wishes to become a limited company must, by law, be registered with Companies House.

Competitive advantage: an advantage a business has that enables it to perform better than its rivals in the market and which is both distinctive and defensible.

Competitive environment: is a market where there are many businesses selling similar goods and services.

Computer aided design (CAD): using computers in the design or modelling process of components or goods.

Computer aided manufacture (CAM): using computers to control machines and equipment.

Consumer: the person who ultimately uses (or consumes) a product.

Consumer income: the amount of money consumers have left to spend after they have paid their taxes and living expenses.

Consumer Rights Act: an Act that protects the public's buying rights when purchasing goods and services.

Consumer spending: the amount of money consumers have to spend.

Contribution per unit: how much each product made and sold contributes to fixed cost, then profit. Contribution = selling price per unit – variable costs per unit.

Cost of goods sold: costs directly linked with the production of goods or services; the more products or services sold, the higher the variable costs will be. Also known as cost of goods sold.

Costs: the expenses and bills a business has to pay.

Crowdfunding: when a business attracts a crowd of investors from the Internet, each of whom takes a small stake by contributing towards an online fundraising target.

Customers: any individuals or organisations who buy or are supplied with a product by a business.

Customer engagement: the means by which a business creates a connection between its customer base and the experiences of customers with the business.

Customer needs: the wants and desires of buyers of a product or the customers of a business.

Customer reviews: information direct from customers, of their thoughts and feelings about a product or service.

CV: a document an applicant creates that is a summary of their personal, career, education and skills details.

Decentralised: where business decisions are made at a local level, by local managers rather than centrally by senior managers.

Decline phase: the final phase of the product life cycle; products become outdated as tastes and technology change.

Demographics: statistical data relating to the population and particular groups within it.

Design mix: the range of variables that contribute to successful design: they are function, cost and appearance.

Development: improving or perfecting existing skills.

Differentiation: making a product/service different from another in some way.

Digital communication: communicating using electronic equipment such as emails, texts, websites.

Direct costs: costs directly linked with the production of goods or services; the more products or services sold, the higher the variable costs will be. Also known as cost of goods sold.

Directors: individuals responsible for companies.

Discrimination: when individuals are treated differently based on their age, race, religion, gender or disability.

Distribution: to get a product to the right place for customers to make their purchases.

Distribution channel: the route that a product takes, from where it is manufactured to where it is sold.

Dividend: a sum of money paid regularly by a company to its shareholders out of its profits.

Dynamic business: businesses that adapt to meet the changing needs of customers and developments in the market.

E-commerce: the activity of buying and selling goods and services online.

Economic climate: the broad performance of the UK economy.

Economies of scale: cost advantages gained by expanding the level of production.

Employees: a person who is hired for a wage, salary, fee or payment to perform work for an employer or business.

End user: the consumer or person who ultimately uses a product.

E-newsletter: a newsletter published electronically.

E-tailer: businesses that sell goods and services through the Internet.

Enterprise: the characteristics and skills needed to start a business and take risks.

Entrepreneur: a person who owns and runs their own business and takes risks.

Ethics: moral guidelines for good behaviour; doing what is morally right.

Exchange rate: the cost of exchanging one currency for another.

Exports: when a business makes products in the UK then sells them to other countries.

Extension strategies: methods used by businesses to prolong the sales of their products, e.g. re-branding, lower price.

External recruitment: when a business hires people from outside the business.

External source of finance: finance that is obtained from outside the business such as bank loans, cash from the issue of shares.

Factors of production: the resources required by an entrepreneur to produce goods and services.

Financial data: past, present and future records of the financial health of a business. This could include financial and accounting records as well as sales, marketing and salary data.

Financial security: being financially independent and not having to rely on others for income.

Fixed costs: costs that remain the same regardless of the level of output, e.g. salaries, advertising, rent.

Flat (organisation): few levels of authority in a business.

Flexible hours: when someone will work the number of hours they are contracted to but with more choice over when they work.

Flow production: a large number of identical components or goods produced together on an assembly line.

Formal training: when a business arranges for staff to have training that has specific objectives. Formal training is provided by specialists and tends to be away from work.

Franchise: the right given by one business to another to sell goods or services using its name.

Franchisee: a business that agrees to manufacture, distribute or provide a branded product, under licence from a franchisor.

Franchisor: the business that gives franchisees the right to sell its product in return for a fixed sum of money or a royalty payment.

Freelance contracts: when someone is self-employed and they choose to work for different businesses on a contract-by-contract basis.

Freemium: a pricing strategy offering an initial product or service for free but which requires a payment for any additional services that are deemed premium.

Fringe benefits: when a business rewards its staff with something of financial value such as the use of a company car, free gym membership or free travel.

Full-time: with regards to employment, staff who work for around 35 hours per week.

Gap in the market: occurs when no business is currently serving the needs of customers for a particular product.

Give notice: when an employee or employer advises the other that they wish to terminate the employment contract.

Globalisation: when organisations and businesses trade internationally.

Goods: physical, tangible products, such as a car, a pair of scissors or a smart phone.

Government: the people and organisations given the authority to govern a country.

Gross Domestic Product (GDP): an estimate of the total value of goods and services produced in a country.

Gross profit: a calculation of how much profit a business makes from selling products or services after it has deducted the cost of sales (costs incurred directly). The formula for gross profit is: sales revenue – cost of sales.

Gross profit margin: the formula for gross profit margin is: gross profit margin – gross profit/sales revenue × 100.

Growth: when a business becomes bigger.

Growth phase: the second phase of the product life cycle; sales grow as awareness of the product and its popularity increases.

Hierarchical: something that relates to levels of authority.

Incorporation: a registered company. Owners have limited liability.

Indirect costs: costs not directly linked with the production of the goods or service being produced and sold.

Informal training: when a business arranges for staff to receive less structured training. Informal training usually takes place within the workplace and involves other team members to provide training.

Imports: when products made overseas are brought into the UK.

Inflation: when prices of goods and services continue to rise.

Inorganic growth: happens when a business conducts a merger (when two businesses join together) or takeover. Also known as external growth.

Insolvency: when a business does not have enough cash to pay its bills when they are due.

Interest rate: the amount charged for borrowing money or as a reward for savings.

Internal recruitment: when a business decides to appoint someone for a job who already works for the business.

Internal source of finance: when a business finds the money from within itself, such as retained profit or the sale of assets.

Internet cookies: data collected by a website and stored on a user's computer that allows the browsing history to be collected so preferences can be applied on future visits.

Introduction phase: the first phase of the product life cycle; the launch of the product.

Jargon: the vocabulary used by an industry/profession/group of people that relates to their area of expertise.

Job application form: form prepared by a business for a candidate to complete when applying for a job.

Job description: a document prepared by a business that explains the responsibilities and duties of a job and the day-to-day tasks related to the job.

Job enrichment: when a business tries to make a job more demanding and less boring in order to motivate staff.

Job production: a production method where one component or good is produced at a time.

Job rotation: staff are given short periods of time on various jobs before they move onto other jobs.

Just in time (JIT): a stock management system where stock is delivered only when needed by the production system, so no stock is kept by the business.

Lead time: the time it takes for new stock to arrive once it has been ordered.

Legislation: laws set by governments that set out a strict set of rules in which businesses can operate and individuals can act.

Level of output: the number of goods or services being produced by an organisation.

Liability: the legal responsibility that a business owner has to pay the debts of the business.

Line managers: workers in charge of staff during their shift; they are normally paid a higher salary for this responsibility.

Limited liability: when a business cannot pay its debts the owners (shareholders) are not liable for the debts of the business. All they will lose is the value of their shares, which they have already paid for.

Loan/loan capital: a cash lump sum borrowed (often from a bank) that the business pays back in regular monthly repayments, with interest added.

Local community: a group of people who live and/or work in a geographical area in which a business operates.

Logistics: management of stock in terms of storage and when being transported.

Long-term sources of finance: borrowing for larger amounts of money that can be repaid over longer periods of time (usually longer than 12 months).

Loss: when outgoings (costs) are higher than revenue (income).

Managers: individuals who are in charge of a certain group of tasks or group of people.

Manufacturer: a person or business that makes goods.

Margin of safety: the difference between the break-even point and the actual level of sales, i.e. output on top of break-even point.

Market conditions: the characteristics of a market, such as how competitive it is and its growth rate.

Market data/marketing data: data that helps a business make decisions based on primary or secondary research.

Market map: a diagram used to position and compare products in a market.

Market research: the process of gaining information about customers, competitors and market trends through collecting primary and secondary data.

Market segment: a part of a market that contains a group of buyers with similar buying habits, such as age or income.

Market segmentation: breaking down a market into smaller groups, which are called segments.

Marketing mix: a combination of factors that help a business to take into account customer needs when selling a product, usually summarised as the 4 Ps – price, place, product, promotion.

Market share: the percentage of sales held by a business in a particular market.

Market trends: anything that alters the market that a business operates in.

Maturity phase: the second phase of the product life cycle; sales of the product peak.

Maximum stock level: the highest amount of stock to be kept by a business.

Merger: when two businesses join together.

Minimum stock level (buffer stock): the minimum amount of stock held by a business.

Motivation: when members of staff want to give their best effort and care about the business they work for.

Multinational companies (MNCs): businesses that operate and trade in more than one country.

Net profit: profit after direct costs and other operating expenses are deducted (such as fixed costs) and bank interest. The formula for net profit is: gross profit – other operating expenses and interest.

Net profit margin: net profit/sales revenue × 100.

Objectives: short-term steps taken by an organisation to help it achieve a long-term aim.

Observation: when an employee watches another member of staff to learn how a job is done; also known as shadowing.

One-off costs: costs that a business has to pay for only once, e.g. buying machinery.

Ongoing training: when staff continue to receive training on a regular basis.

Opening balance: the amount of money a business has in its account at the beginning of an accounting period, e.g. a month, a financial year.

Operational staff: staff hired to look after other day-to-day jobs such as receptionists and administration staff.

Order quantity: the amount or quantity of materials ordered.

Organic growth: when a business grows on its own without merging with or taking over any other business; also known as internal growth.

Organisational structure: a diagram showing the internal structure of a business and the roles and responsibilities of the staff who work for it, displayed in levels of authority.

Overdraft: borrowing money from a bank by drawing more money than is actually in a current account, i.e. spending all of the business's money then dipping into the bank's money. Interest is charged by the bank on the amount overdrawn.

Owners: the people that a business belongs to.

Part-time: with regard to employment, staff who gain the same benefits as full-time staff but work for less than 35 hours per week.

Partnership: between two and 20 people who own a business and have unlimited liability.

Payment systems: the electronic ability to transfer money quickly and safely from one bank account to another.

Performance reviews: when a member of staff meets with their manager to review their work performance.

Permanent contracts: a contract on an ongoing basis or on an until-further-notice basis.

Person specification: a document prepared by a business that explains what they are seeking in any applicant for a job.

Personal satisfaction: an individual's sense of fulfilment of a need or want.

Personal savings: money that belongs to the owner of a business, for personal use.

Piece rate: a method of paying staff according to how many pieces of work they produce/complete.

Place: a location where customers can purchase goods and services.

Post-sales service: the procedures that a business has in place to support customers after the sale of a good or service.

Pressure groups: groups of people who want to ensure businesses and governments act ethically in relation to the environment/animal welfare/human rights.

Price: the amount that customers have to pay for a product.

Pricing strategy: the plan for setting a product's price.

Primary research: the gathering of new information, called primary data, which has not been collected before; also called field research.

Primary sector: companies and people working to extract raw materials from the earth or the sea.

Private limited company (Ltd): a type of privately held small business. This type of business entity limits owner liability to their shares, limits the number of shareholders to 50, and restricts shareholders from publicly trading the company's shares.

Procurement: the act of obtaining or buying raw materials, components or services from a supplier to be used in the production of goods and services.

Product: term used to describe goods or services.

Product differentiation: making one product different from another in some way, for instance through the quality of its design, packaging or advertising.

Product life cycle: the stages through which a product passes from its development to being withdrawn from sale. The phases are research and development; launching the product; growth; maturity; saturation and decline.

Product range: a group of similar products made by a business, like a number of different chocolate bars.

Product trial: used to get customers to try a product for the first time, usually before a business decides to launch it fully to the market.

Production costs: the costs associated with producing goods and services.

Production process: transforming raw materials or inputs into finished products.

Productivity: measures output per worker (or machine) over a period of time.

Profit: where the revenues of a business are greater than its costs over a period of time. Profit = selling price – total costs.

Profitability: how good a business is at making a profit, not simply how much profit they have made.

Promotion (of employee): when an employee rises up the hierarchy of an organisation.

Promotion strategy: a plan to identify the most appropriate promotion methods for a good or service.

Public Limited Company (plc): a company whose shares can be bought and sold on the stock market.

Public relations: promotion of a positive image about a product or business through giving information about the product to the general public, other businesses or to the press.

Qualitative data: information about opinions, judgements and attitudes.

Quality: achieving a minimum standard for a product or service or a production process, which meets customer needs.

Quality assurance: ensuring that quality is produced and delivered at every stage of the production process, often through making quality the responsibility of every worker involved.

Quality control: ensuring that a product or service meets minimum standards, often through testing of sample products once they have been made.

Quantitative data: data that can be expressed as numbers and statistically analysed.

Quantitative business data: numerical and statistical data.

Raw materials: substances used as an input to a production process for manufacturing into finished goods. Sometimes referred to as commodities.

Re-order level: the amount of stock held by a business at which an order for new stock is placed with suppliers.

Remote working: people working together from different locations, whether from home or even from different countries.

Remuneration: financial payment for an employee for completion of work.

Repeat purchase: when a customer buys a product more than once – they return to buy a product again.

Retailer: a business which specialises in selling goods in small quantities to the consumer.

Retained profit: profits that a business has made from previous years of trading.

Revenue: the amount of money/cash coming into a business from selling products over a period of time.

Rewards: the advantages of a course of action, including benefits to an owner.

Risks: the chances of damage or loss occurring as a result of making a decision.

Sale of assets: when a business sells something physical of value to raise capital, e.g. machinery, vehicles, equipment.

Sales: the amount of products or services that are being sold. Sales can also be another word for revenue or income.

Sales process: the steps a business or individual goes through in order to maximise sales of a good or service.

Sales revenue: how much a business receives in payment from selling goods and services to customers.

Secondary research: the process of gathering secondary data, which is information that has already been gathered such as sales records, governments statistics, newspaper reports, Internet or reports from market research groups. Also known as desk research.

Secondary sector: businesses that transform raw materials into finished goods.

Self-learning: when an employee studies without the presence of a teacher or colleague.

Senior managers: responsible for the day-to-day operations of the business in order for the aims and objectives of the business to be achieved.

Services: non-physical, intangible products, e.g. a taxi journey, a haircut, a TV programme.

Share capital: when a registered company sells shares to raise finance in exchange for a share in profits.

Shareholders: people who have bought shares in a business to receive a share in future profits.

Short-term sources of finance: small amounts of borrowing, which must be repaid within one year.

SMART: stands for: specific, measurable, achievable, realistic and timely. SMART is used for objective setting for a business.

Social media: Internet-based forms of communication, e.g. Twitter, Facebook, Instagram.

Social objectives: providing goods and services that are kind to the environment or benefit a community.

Sole trader: the only owner of a business; she/he has unlimited liability.

Staff turnover: the percentage of staff who leave a business during a certain period of time.

Stakeholders: any person who has an interest in a business and/or is affected by the activities of a business.

Stakeholder conflict: when different stakeholders disagree on business decisions that affect them.

Stock: materials that a business holds. Some stock can be materials waiting to be used in the production process and some can be finished stock waiting to be delivered to customers.

Stock market flotation: when a business becomes a public limited company (plc) and raises capital by inviting members of the public to buy shares in the business.

Supervisors: individuals who work with staff and have the authority to delegate work, reward and discipline staff. Also known as team leaders.

Suppliers: businesses that sell (or supply) products to other businesses.

Support staff: carry out specific jobs which help facilitate business success, such as computer (IT) technicians, caretakers and canteen staff.

Survival: an aim for an organisation to be able to simply survive in a competitive environment, especially new businesses. Profit may come later.

Sustainable: to make something last longer.

Takeover: when one large business buys a smaller business.

Target market: a specific group of customers (segment) at which a business aims its products.

Tariffs: a tax added onto the selling price of an imported good so that it makes it more expensive to buy in the UK.

Tax: a percentage of profits, income or revenue imposed by the government and paid to the government.

Temporary contracts: workers who have no permanent contract of employment with a business and so tend to work only for a short period of time for an employer, e.g. supply teacher.

Tertiary sector: companies or people who provide services.

Total costs: when fixed costs and variable costs are added together.

Trade barriers: when a government deliberately restricts opportunities, efficiency and competition for importers in order to protect their own country's businesses against global competition.

Trade blocs: when certain countries group together and agree to make it easier for the members of their group to market for goods, services, capital, and labour by getting rid of all barriers to trade.

Trade credit: when a business receives goods from a supplier now but agrees to pay for the goods at a later date.

Trade-off: a compromise between one thing and another when it is not possible to have both things at the same time.

Trading Standards Authority: a body that checks that businesses adhere to strict rules when selling goods and services in order to protect the public from being sold counterfeits.

Training: the action of teaching a person new skills.

Unemployment: when there are not enough jobs for people who are willing and able to work.

Unique selling points: characteristics of a product that make it different from other similar products being sold in the market, e.g. design, quality or image. Also referred to as USPs.

Unlimited liability: where the owner of a business has a legal obligation to pay all the business's debts. If the owner can't pay these debts, the creditor can take possession of the owner's goods, house, etc. and sell them to cover the debt. The business and the owner are deemed to be one and the same entity.

Variable costs: costs that increase as level of output increases, e.g. raw materials, electricity, temporary worker wages.

Venture capital: when external investors with extensive business experience are willing to invest considerable funds into a business at their own risk.

Viral advertising: getting individuals to spread the message about a product through social media networks such as Facebook or their groups of friends.

Viral marketing: when a business uses social media to encourage the public to share information about its goods and services.

Wages: employees paid on an hourly rate.

Wholesaler: a business that buys in bulk from a manufacturer or other supplier and then sells the stock on in smaller quantities to retailers.

Index

Collins

Edexcel GCSE 9-1
Business

Workbook

Stephanie Campbell, Helen Kellaway
and Tony Michaelides

Contents

Investigating Small Business

Building a Business

Exam Papers

Revision Tips

Rethink Revision

Have you ever taken part in a quiz and thought '*I know this*!', but, despite frantically racking your brain, you just couldn't come up with the answer?

It's very frustrating when this happens, but in a fun situation it doesn't really matter. However, in your GCSE exams, it will be essential that you can recall the relevant information quickly when you need to.

Most students think that revision is about making sure you **know** stuff. Of course, this is important, but it is also about becoming confident that you can **retain** that *stuff* over time and **recall** it quickly when needed.

Revision That Really Works

Experts have discovered that there are two techniques that help with all of these things and consistently produce better results in exams compared to other revision techniques.

Applying these techniques to your GCSE revision will ensure you get better results in your exams and will have all the relevant knowledge at your fingertips when you start studying for further qualifications, like AS and A Levels, or begin work.

It really isn't rocket science either – you simply need to:

* **test yourself** on each topic as many times as possible
* **leave a gap** between the test sessions.

It is most effective if you leave a good period of time between the test sessions, e.g. between a week and a month. The idea is that just as you start to forget the information, you force yourself to recall it again, keeping it fresh in your mind.

Three Essential Revision Tips

1. **Use Your Time Wisely**
    * Allow yourself plenty of time.
    * Try to start revising six months before your exams – it's more effective and less stressful.
    * Your revision time is precious so use it wisely – using the techniques described on this page will ensure you revise effectively and efficiently and get the best results.
    * Don't waste time re-reading the same information over and over again – it's time-consuming and not effective!

2. **Make a Plan**
    * Identify all the topics you need to revise (this All-in-One Revision & Practice book will help you).
    * Plan at least five sessions for each topic.
    * One hour should be ample time to test yourself on the key ideas for a topic.
    * Spread out the practice sessions for each topic – the optimum time to leave between each session is about one month but, if this isn't possible, just make the gaps as big as realistically possible.

3. **Test Yourself**
    * Methods for testing yourself include: quizzes, practice questions, flashcards, past papers, explaining a topic to someone else, etc.
    * This All-in-One Revision & Practice book provides seven practice opportunities per topic.
    * Don't worry if you get an answer wrong – provided you check what the correct answer is, you are more likely to get the same or similar questions right in future!

Visit our website to download your free flashcards, for more information about the benefits of these revision techniques, and for further guidance on how to plan ahead and make them work for you.

www.collins.co.uk/collinsGCSErevision

Enterprise and Entrepreneurship

1 What does the term 'gap in the market' mean?

.... [1]

2 Which **one** of the following best describes an original idea?

    A An idea that fills a gap in the market to meet customers' needs that no other business is meeting   ☐

    B An idea that is obsolete   ☐

    C A new version of an old product   ☐

    D Providing a cheaper service than competitors   ☐   [1]

3 Give an example of how consumer tastes have changed.

.... [1]

4 Why is it important that an entrepreneur is not deterred by the risks of starting a small business?

....

....

.... [3]

5 Give examples of how changes in technology have benefited consumers.

....

....

.... [3]

6 At what stage of a business should an entrepreneur aim to consider potential risks?

.... [1]

7 In business, what is meant by the term 'service'?

.... [1]

8 Which **one** of the following is a benefit of adding value?

A Losing market share ☐

B Independence ☐

C Charging a higher price ☐

D Increased costs ☐ [1]

9 Explain why a business must find out about customer needs.

....

....

.... [3]

10 What does the term 'added value' mean?

....

.... [1]

11 Explain why success means different things to different entrepreneurs.

....

....

.... [3]

12 Why does starting a business present a financial risk for the owner?

....

.... [2]

Spotting a Business Opportunity

1 Why is it important for a business to adapt to meet customer needs?

_____

_____

_____ [3]

2 Why is it important for businesses to offer value for money?

_____

_____

_____ [3]

3 What are the rewards satisfied customers bring to a business?

_____

_____

_____ [3]

4 What is meant by the term 'market research'?

_____

_____ [1]

5 Give **two** benefits of conducting market research.

_____

_____ [2]

Spotting a Business Opportunity

6 Give **three** disadvantages of primary research.

....

....

.... [3]

7 What does a business need to consider before using market research?

....

....

.... [3]

8 Give **three** benefits of using social media to collect market research.

....

....

.... [3]

SOCIAL MEDIA

9 What are the **five** main ways in which a business can segment (divide) its market?

....

....

....

....

....

[5]

10 Give **two** examples of features that can be used on a market map.

....

....

[2]

11 What are the **five** ways businesses compete with each other?

....

....

....

....

....

[5]

12 Name **one** drawback to a business of competing through customer service.

....

....

[1]

Putting a Business Idea into Practice

1 Outline the meaning of the term 'cash-flow forecast'.

....

.... [2]

2 Outline the meaning of the term 'cash surplus'.

....

.... [2]

3 Daisy Chain is a small florist shop that specialises in fresh locally grown flowers.

a) From the cash-flow statement below, calculate the net cash-flow for February and March.

	February	March
Opening balance	£15 000	
Cash inflow	£12 000	£15 000
Cash outflow	£13 000	£13 500
Closing balance	£14 000	

....

.... [2]

b) What is the opening balance and closing balance for the month of March?

.... [2]

4 Daisy Chain has the following figures in June and July.

a) Complete the table with the **five** missing figures.

	June (£)	July (£)
Receipts	27 400	
Raw materials	7300	6900
Fixed costs	2600	
Total costs	9900	9500
Net cash-flow		16 300
Opening balance	21 300	
Closing balance		55 100

[5]

b) Calculate Daisy Chain's total costs for August if their bill for raw materials costs is 10% higher than in July.

_____

_____ [2]

c) Explain **one** benefit for Daisy Chain of creating a cash-flow forecast.

_____

_____

_____ [3]

d) Explain why cash is vital for Daisy Chain.

_____

_____

_____ [3]

e) Explain how Daisy Chain could benefit from trade credit from its suppliers.

_____

_____

_____ [3]

f) Name **one** disadvantage of trade credit for Daisy Chain.

_____ [1]

g) How might Daisy Chain benefit from arranging an overdraft facility?

_____

_____

_____ [3]

h) Name **two** disadvantages for Daisy Chain if it were to use an overdraft facility.

_____

_____ [2]

Making the Business Effective

1 Rebecca is an entrepreneur and wants to open a smoothie bar in her local shopping centre. She has personal savings that she does not want to lose if her business isn't successful. Rebecca has a friend who is eager to be part of the business and is brilliant with accounts.

Would you recommend that Rebecca starts her business as a partnership or as a private limited company?

Explain your answer.

_____

_____

_____

_____

_____ [4]

2 What is meant by a sole trader?
Use an example in your answer.

_____

_____ [2]

Making the Business Effective

3 Explain **two** disadvantages of starting a private limited company.

[2]

4 What is meant by the term 'business location'?

[1]

5 What are the **five** factors that should be considered when a business chooses a location?

[5]

6 Explain why location is important for a business in the secondary sector.

[2]

7 How has the Internet made an impact on the product element of the marketing mix?

[1]

8 How does modifying each element in the marketing mix enable a business to remain competitive?

[1]

Making the Business Effective

9 State **one** purpose of promotion.

.... [1]

10 Give **one** reason why an entrepreneur would produce a business plan.

.... [1]

11 How does a business plan help to ensure an entrepreneur has direction?

....

....

.... [3]

12 What information do banks and lenders want to see within a business plan?

....

.... [2]

13 Why don't all businesses need a business plan?

....

.... [2]

Understanding External Influences on Business

1 What is a pressure group?

....

.... [2]

2 Explain **one** way in which the government is a stakeholder in a business.

....

....

....

.... [3]

3 What are electronic payment systems?

....

.... [2]

4 Give **two** examples of digital communication.

....

.... [2]

5 What does the Health and Safety Act ensure for workers?

.... [1]

6 A consumer is entitled to buy products of satisfactory quality.
What does 'satisfactory quality' mean?

.... [2]

7 What are the benefits to the economy of high levels of employment?

....

....

.... [3]

Understanding External Influences on Business

8 Explain how a business can benefit from a recession when recruiting staff.

....

....

.... [3]

9 What are interest rates?

....

.... [2]

10 What is the role of the Advertising Standards Authority (ASA)?

....

.... [2]

11 When interest rates increase, what tends to happen to consumer spending, and why?

....

....

.... [3]

12 What does the acronym SPICED stand for?

.... [1]

Growing the Business

1 Explain **one** benefit for a business of it growing organically.

_____

_____

_____ [3]

2 What does the term 'takeover' mean?

_____

_____ [2]

3 List **three** disadvantages of selling assets as a way of raising finance for a business.

_____

_____

_____

_____ [3]

4 Give an example of when technology has changed the aims and objectives of a business.

_____ [1]

5 Give an example of when a business may change the size of its workforce as a method of achieving its objectives.

_____ [1]

6 What is a Multinational Company (MNC)?

_____ [1]

7 What is a tariff?

_____

_____ [2]

8 How has globalisation helped e-commerce?

....

.... [2]

9 What is the meaning of the term 'boycott'?

.... [1]

10 What is the meaning of the term 'trade off'?
Give an example.

.... [1]

Making Marketing Decisions

1 What is the name given to the element of the design mix that refers to the amount a business spends on producing a product?

.... [1]

2 Why may businesses not make a profit during the introduction stage of the product life cycle?

....

....

....

.... [4]

3 How does operating in a competitive environment impact the pricing decisions of a business?

....

.... [1]

4 How will a business price a product with little differentiation?

.... [1]

5 How do businesses make decisions on the most appropriate promotion strategy?

....

.... [2]

6 Give an example of a special offer for a mass market product.

.... [1]

7 Explain how retailers get products to customers.

....

.... [2]

Making Marketing Decisions

8 Explain **one** benefit e-tailers bring to customers.

....

....

....   [3]

9 Give an example of how a business uses place to gain a competitive advantage.

....

....   [1]

10 Explain how the promotion element of the marketing mix influences product.

....

....

....   [3]

11 What are the **five** factors that will influence a business achieving an integrated marketing mix?

....

....

....

....

....   [5]

12 How can a business use price to gain a competitive advantage?

....   [1]

Making Operational Decisions

1 Explain the job production process.

....

.... [2]

2 Explain **one** disadvantage of flow production.

....

....

.... [2]

3 How does batch production achieve lower unit costs for businesses?

....

.... [2]

4 What is just in time stock control?

....

....

.... [3]

5 What is the impact on a business of having too little stock?

....

.... [2]

6 Why is quality an important factor when choosing a supplier?

....

.... [2]

Making Operational Decisions

7 What is the difference between quality control and quality assurance?

....

....

.... [2]

8 How do effective quality management systems reduce the cost of production?

....

.... [2]

9 How do customer expectations influence the quality standards businesses set?

....

....

.... [3]

10 How can sales people help customers to make good purchasing choices?

....

.... [2]

11 Why is customer feedback an important part of the sales process?

....

....

.... [2]

12 Outline **one** way a business benefits from offering good customer service.

....

.... [1]

Making Financial Decisions

1 What are direct costs?

....

.... [1]

2 What is the formula for gross profit?

.... [1]

3 What is the formula for net profit/loss?

.... [1]

4 Pepper Pizzas have monthly fixed costs of £930 and variable costs of £1.80 per pizza. The selling price of each pizza is £8.

Calculate the net profit or loss that Pepper Pizza will make if it sells the entire stock of 400 pizzas in one week.

Show your workings and the formula used.

....

....

....

.... [3]

Making Financial Decisions

5 Why are profit and profitability not the same thing?

....

....
[2]

6 What would a low gross profit margin indicate to a business?

....

....
[1]

7 What does the calculation 'average rate of return' (ARR) show an investor?

....

....
[2]

8 What is the formula for average rate of return (ARR)?

....
[1]

9 What is financial data?

....
[1]

10 Suggest **two** ways financial data can be used.

....

....
[1]

Making Human Resource Decisions

1 Name a disadvantage of a business with a centralised organisation.

.... [1]

2 Name **two** benefits to a business of effective communication.

....

.... [1]

3 What are flexible working hours?

.... [1]

4 What are supervisors?

.... [1]

5 Name **two** methods a business could use to advertise an internal job.

....

.... [2]

6 What does a CV show?

.... [1]

7 What could be a benefit of a business issuing application forms for applicants to complete, rather than asking for CVs?

....

.... **[2]**

8 Identify **one** advantage of informal training.

.... **[1]**

9 Why might a business want to train and develop staff?

.... **[1]**

10 When would an employee receive commission?

.... **[1]**

11 What is job rotation?

....

.... **[1]**

Collins

GCSE Edexcel Business
Paper 1: Investigating small business

Time: 1 hour 30 minutes

Instructions

- Use **black** ink or black ball-point pen.
- **Fill in the boxes** at the bottom of this page.
- There are **three** sections in this paper.
- Answer **all** questions. You must answer the questions in the spaces provided.
- Calculators may be used.
- You are advised to **show all your working out** with **your answer clearly shown** at **the end**.

Information

- The total mark for this paper is 90.
- The marks for **each** question are shown in brackets – **use this as a guide as to how much time you should spend on each question**.

Advice

- You must read the questions provided with care before attempting to answer.
- Make every attempt to answer all questions provided.
- If you have time, check your answers.

Section A

Answer ALL questions.
Write your answers in the spaces provided.

Some questions must be answered with a cross in a box ☒. If you change your mind about an answer, put a line through the box ☒ and then mark your new answer with a cross ☒.

---

0 1 **(a)** Which **one** of the following is an example of a cash inflow?

Select **one** answer. (1)

☒ **A** Sales

☐ **B** Wages

☐ **C** Loan repayments

☐ **D** Stock

(b) Which **one** of the following is not an example of primary research?

Select **one** answer. (1)

☐ **A** Survey

☐ **B** Focus group

☒ **C** Newspaper articles

☐ **D** Interview

(c) Explain **one** benefit to a business of having effective customer service. (3)

By a business having an effective customer service as customer will more likley re-buy items and become a loyal customer which would help to increce the revenu.

(d) Explain **one** advantage of having limited liability. (3)

....

....

....

....

....

(Total for Question 1 = 8 marks)

Practice Exam Paper 1

0 2 **(a)** What is implementing a new product into an already existing market called?

Select **one** answer. **(1)**

- [X] **A** Innovation
- [ ] **B** Entrepreneurship
- [ ] **C** Enterprise
- [ ] **D** Invention

(b) Which **two** of the following are examples of goods?

Select **two** answers. **(2)**

- [X] **A** Mobile phone
- [ ] **B** Haircut
- [ ] **C** Doctors appointment
- [X] **D** Suit
- [ ] **E** Bus journey

The cash-flow forecast for a small business is shown below.

(c) Complete the **five** missing figures in the table. **(5)**

	November (£)	**December (£)**
Total receipts	18 400	20200
Stock	7050	10 000
Fixed costs	3200	3200
Total payments	10 250	13200
Net cash-flow	8150	7000
Opening balance	5400	13 550
Closing balance	13550	20550

(d) Explain **one** method a business could use to add value to a chocolate bar.　　(3)

A business could add value by convinece like dilivery to a door as the consumer will be more ~~likly~~ likley to pay more for the convinces and dilivery of the product allowing a business to rais prices and have good Customer Satisfaction.

(e) Which of the following is most likely to increase a business's profit?

Select **one** answer.　　(1)

☒ **A** Lower stock costs

☐ **B** Fewer customers

☐ **C** Higher labour costs

☐ **D** Lower productivity

(Total for Question 2 = 12 marks)

0 3 (a) Which **one** of the following sources of long-term finance is suitable for a private limited company? (1)

- [×] A Trade credit
- [ ] B Overdraft
- [ ] C Factoring
- [×] D Share capital

(b) Using the information below calculate the total cost for the small business. Ensure you show any relevant workings. (2)

Quantity sold: 500

Fixed costs: £2000

Variable costs per unit: £1.50

$$2000 + (500 \times 1.50) = 2750$$

(c) Explain **one** possible conflict of interest between a customer and the shareholders of a business. (3)

One conflict of intrest between a customer and the shareholders of a business could be the price of a product as the shareholder will want to rise the price to get more money but a customer will not want that so its more afferdable.

(d) Explain **one** advantage to customers of a competitive market. (3)

An advantage to a customer of a competetive market is that there are lots of opptions so the customer has lots to pick from and has the best option of price, pto and quality but also asthetic

(e) Justify what a business must consider when deciding upon the prices offered for their products. (6)

(Total for Question 3 = 15 marks)

TOTAL FOR SECTION A = 35 MARKS

Practice Exam Paper 1

Section B

Answer ALL questions.
Write your answers in the spaces provided.

Read the text below carefully then answer Questions 4, 5 and 6.

Peter Harris owns and runs a shop called Harris's Celebrations, which sells cards for various occasions including birthdays, weddings and religious festivals. His shop is located in a busy town centre with excellent transport links. The cards are considered to be high-quality with unique designs and materials used to make the products.

The business has been running for eight months and the revenue has steadily increased month on month. Customers are travelling from various locations to purchase the cards thanks to the unique selling point of the products. Due to this, during peak holiday seasons such as Christmas the store becomes very busy and customers have to form large queues in order to purchase the cards from Peter.

A combination of high demand and an inability to cope with the number of customers in the store is making Peter consider expanding his business and setting up a website so that customers can purchase the products without visiting the store. The website would also allow the ability to see the full range of products offered by Harris's Celebrations.

One customer mentioned "The quality of the cards is fantastic. I have yet to find another card company with as high-quality cards as Harris's Celebrations. However, the experience of the store is horrible during peak times because you can hardly move in the store, as it gets extremely busy."

0 4 **(a)** Outline **one** method of primary research Peter could use to help gather information about his customers. **(2)**

> He could go to social media to get the publics oppions and wants for the shop so he can learn how to improve his customer survice.

(b) Analyse the impact on Harris's Celebrations of Peter opening up a website to help cope with demand for the cards in his store. **(6)**

> This would have a positive impact as the store will be able to access more people widly helping him sell to a wider market increasing revenue and profit. However it can icrease the costs for Harris and make him spend more time working effecting him.
>
> By also opening up a website it will help to impreve the experience at the store during peak seasons as less people will have to go in the store increasing the sales customere experence making them want to go back & so he gets more sales.

(Total for Question 4 = 8 marks)

0 5 (a) Outline **one** benefit of having high-quality cards in Peter's store. (2)

improve reputation.

> By having high quality peter can charge more for the cards which will help to increase revenu as people will be willing & to pay this.

To create the website, it is going to cost £5000. Unfortunately for Peter he does not have this money and will need to borrow the money from a bank. He will pay the loan over two years and will have a monthly repayment of £225.

(b) Calculate the total interest Peter will have to pay for the loan.
Show your workings. (2)

> 225 x24 = 5400   12 x 2 = 24
>
> 5400 - 5000 = £400
>
> $\frac{400}{5000}$ = 8%

(c) Assess whether Peter should use a bank loan to fund his new website for the business. **(6)**

Peter should use a bank loan to fund his website as he could get advice from the banker to help him improve his website and make it better but it also means he wont lose anything, like his personal savings making this good and effective

However it takes a long time to get a bank loan making it not efficent for him but also the monthly payments will reduce his revenu making it not the best opption for him to take.

(Total for Question 5 = 10 marks)

0 6 Peter has fixed costs of £10 000. His selling price is £3 and his variable cost per unit is £1.

(a) Calculate the break-even point. (3)

~~£10 000~~ 5000 units

Peter is going to consider **two** options to increase the revenue for his business.

Option 1: Increased advertisement

Option 2: Reduce prices

(b) Justify which of these options Peter should implement. (9)

Peter should increase advertisment to help
                                   across
get his ~~a~~ unique selling point^which
will help him to get more sales as people
will be able to see what they are buying.

By increasing advertisment it will help Peter
to be more seen and allow more people to
discover his high quality shop ~~will~~ which
will increase his market and revenu.

(Total for Question 6 = 12 marks)

TOTAL FOR SECTION B = 30 MARKS

Section C

Answer ALL questions.
Write your answers in the spaces provided.

Courtney works in an ice-cream shop in his local area. He is highly talented at making ice-cream and has created many innovative flavours; ingredients Courtney regularly uses include milk, sugar, vegetable oil, salt, cocoa butter and almonds. After working in the shop for several years, he considers starting his own ice-cream shop. Courtney then conducts market research and finds that ice-cream shops have become increasingly popular.

The market is already very competitive, with three main businesses in the local area. However, Courtney has spotted a gap in the market offering low-calorie ice-cream that is of a higher quality than his competitors. Courtney is looking to charge £4 per ice-cream, which is slightly more expensive than his competitors, who all charge £3.75. His research indicates that customers are demanding more sweet treats that are low in calories; this demand is not being met by the existing competition.

Courtney has worked his way up in the business he works for and is currently the store manager. He would be able to raise a significant amount of money to start up his business but would still need a loan. As ice-cream is a luxury item, Courtney is worried that a downturn in the economy may reduce the number of ice-cream sales.

| 0 7 | (a) State **one** element of the marketing mix. | (1)

price

(b) State **one** variable cost an ice-cream maker may have and explain how this might change throughout the year. (3)

Raw matirials is a veriable cost as there will be diffrent demands in each season, with in summer demand will go up increasing the need for more raw matirials to make the icecream

(c) Discuss whether Courtney should start his business as a sole trader instead of a private limited company. (9)

Courtney should start his business as sole trader as he will get complete freedom of the business as well as getting to pick his own hours but also getting to keep all of the profit for himself. But if the business fails he will be leaglly responceible ~~of~~ for all the debts owned but he" has got

expirence and has done market reasearch to prevent this out come

expencive to set up

However plcs are good as it means Courtney has a sepret identiy to the business so ~~if~~ it does fail ~~the~~ Courtny wont be at risk of losing his home. By having a plc ~~raising money~~ raising money can be made as he can sell shares to help out with the starting costs so his loan will be less. But this will decrease his profit

In conclution ~~courrnt~~ Courtney should set his business up as a sole trader as he has the ↑ experence and has conducted the ressecary primary reaseerch to hot fail but also he gets lots of benifits.

(d) Using the information provided, evaluate whether Courtney is right to pursue the idea of his business. (12)

i recommend & that Courtney should pursue the idea of his business as he sees a good gap in the market which he has expirence in which he would ~~get~~ be incharge of his hours, tasks and the business making him fully incontrel of his self.

However by doing this he's taking a big risk for a preduct that is seasonal which could suggest his sales may not be very high as people wont want to eat ice-cream as much in december effecting his revenu at times. It's also likly to suffer as it's a ~~toxty~~ luxary item ~~h~~ so when the economy is low so is sales.

He will also have a unique selling point with his innovated ice cream flavers that he has made which will increase his costermers and stand out from the local compertition.

(Total for Question 7 = 25 marks)

TOTAL FOR SECTION C = 25 MARKS

TOTAL FOR PAPER = 90 MARKS

Collins

GCSE Edexcel Business
Paper 2: Building a business

Time: 1 hour 30 minutes

Instructions

- Use **black** ink or black ball-point pen.
- **Fill in the boxes** at the bottom of this page.
- There are **three** sections in this paper.
- Answer **all** questions. You must answer the questions in the spaces provided.
- Calculators may be used.
- You are advised to **show all your working** with **your answer clearly shown** at **the end**.

Information

- The maximum mark for this paper is 90.
- The marks for **each** question are shown in brackets – **use this as a guide as to how much time you should spend on each question.**

Advice

- You must read the questions provided with care before attempting to answer.
- Make every attempt to answer all questions provided.
- If you have time, check your answers.

Section A

Answer ALL questions.
Write your answers in the spaces provided.

Some questions must be answered with a cross in a box ☒. If you change your mind about an answer, put a line through the box ☒ and then mark your new answer with a cross ☒.

---

0 1 **(a)** Which **one** of the following is not an element of the marketing mix?

Select **one** answer.

(1)

☒ **A** Profit

☐ **B** Place

☐ **C** Price

☐ **D** Promotion

(b) Which **one** of the following is the last stage of the product life cycle?

Select **one** answer.

(1)

☒ **A** Decline

☐ **B** Growth

☐ **C** Maturity

☐ **D** Saturation

(c) Explain **one** benefit to a business of having an effective design mix. (3)

An effective design mix can increase sales as it allows a ~~touis~~ business to perform better. as it gives it a unique selling point.

(d) Explain **one** advantage of on-the-job training. (3)

Job is cheaper as they can ~~te~~ learn on the ~~decay~~ day lowing costs

(Total for Question 1 = 8 marks)

Practice Exam Paper 2

0 2 **(a)** Which **two** of these is not a feature of a public limited company? (2)

Select **two** answers.

- [ ] **A** Limited liability
- [ ] **B** Owners are called shareholders
- [ ] **C** Owners receive dividends
- [ ] **D** Accounts do not have to be displayed to the public
- [ ] **E** Unlimited liability

(b) Which **two** of the following are examples of quality assurance?

Select **two** answers. (2)

- [ ] **A** Quality is checked at every stage of production
- [ ] **B** Quality is checked at the end of the production
- [ ] **C** Quality is everyone's responsibility
- [ ] **D** Only a small amount of defected products
- [ ] **E** High quality products

The table below contains financial information about a business.

Sales	£220 000
Cost of sales	£120 000
Gross profit	£100 000
Overheads	£45 000
Net profit	£55 000

(c) Calculate the net profit margin for the business.
You are recommended to show your workings. (2)

....

....

(d) Explain **one** barrier to communication a business may face. (3)

_____

_____

_____

_____

_____

(e) Explain **one** disadvantage of holding higher levels of buffer stock. (3)

_____

_____

_____

_____

_____

(Total for Question 2 = 12 marks)

Practice Exam Paper 2

0 3 **(a)** Which **one** of the following is an example of an external source of finance? **(1)**

Select **one** answer.

☐ **A** Personal savings

☐ **B** Loan

☐ **C** Retained profit

☐ **D** Selling assets

(b) Using the information below, calculate the total revenue for two months for the following business.

Ensure you show any relevant workings. **(2)**

Selling price of product: £50

Month	Sales volume
January	200
February	300

....

....

....

....

....

(c) Explain **one** reason why a shop selling cars may pay its workers commission. **(3)**

....

....

....

....

....

(d) Explain **one** benefit of a motivated workforce. (3)

(e) Discuss the benefits to the business of using a hierarchical organisational structure. (6)

(Total for Question 3 = 15 marks)

TOTAL FOR SECTION A = 35 MARKS

Section B

Answer ALL questions.
Write your answers in the spaces provided.

Read the text below carefully then answer Questions 4, 5 and 6.

Shaketastic is an established British private limited company that has stores in several London locations. Shaketastic has dessert lounges that offer a wide product range including milkshakes, fruit juices, smoothies and cakes, which use high-quality ingredients. The products are manufactured using fresh produce made directly in front of the customer. The customers are able to customise the products to their requirements, selecting ingredients they would like in their milkshake or smoothie. Shaketastic also produces milkshakes using popular chocolate flavours such as Snickers, Nutella and Oreos, which are instantly recognisable by customers.

Shaketastic also has a mobile phone application where customers are able to order products and have them delivered to their door. Shaketastic also uses social media through Instagram and Twitter to promote the company and the products on offer.

0 4 **(a)** Outline **one** impact of using social media to promote the products. (2)

....

....

....

....

(b) Analyse the impact of Shaketastic charging a higher price for its products. **(6)**

....

....

....

....

....

....

....

....

....

....

....

(Total for Question 4 = 8 marks)

Practice Exam Paper 2

0 5 **(a)** Outline **one** benefit of using brand names in the milkshakes Shaketastic sell to their customers. **(2)**

....

....

....

....

....

(b) Outline **one** limitation of higher buffer stock for Shaketastic. **(2)**

....

....

....

....

(c) Assess what type of production method Shaketastic should use in order to produce their milkshakes. **(6)**

....

....

....

....

....

....

....

....

....

(Total for Question 5 = 10 marks)

0 6 **(a)** State the formula for calculating total cost. (1)

....

(b) Outline **one** possible limitation of Shaketastic delivering products to its customers. (2)

....

....

....

There are two options to increase profit for Shaketastic.

Option 1: Offer a wider range of products

Option 2: Order cheaper raw materials

(c) Justify which of these options Shaketastic should implement. (9)

....

....

....

....

....

....

....

....

....

....

....

(Total for Question 6 = 12 marks)

TOTAL FOR SECTION B = 30 MARKS

Practice Exam Paper 2

Section C

Answer ALL questions.
Write your answers in the spaces provided.

Tesco has recently recorded its greatest loss in the UK. Tesco has removed 5000 head office and store management jobs as a result of its poor performance. It has also closed 43 stores, resulting in 2500 job losses. Analysts have suggested that Tesco let its prices rise too highly and allowed shopfloor standards to fall. One of the reasons for Tesco's decline is that customers have turned to discounters Aldi and Lidl who offer much more competitive prices, with customers seeing little difference in the quality of the products.

However, some customers are coming back to Tesco since it recently cut its prices and improved store service. Tesco now employs fewer staff in management roles but more staff in stores in order to ensure that customer needs are being met. However, Aldi and Lidl are showing no slow down in growth and have significantly increased their sales and market share.

0 7 (a) Name **one** market segment. (1)

(b) Define the term 'customer'. (1)

(c) Outline **one** benefit of Tesco increasing the quality of its products. (2)

In order to make Tesco more competitive against Lidl and Aldi, it has two options:

Option 1: Employ fewer staff

Option 2: Outsource its production to cheaper manufacturers abroad

(d) Justify which of these options Tesco should implement. (9)

(e) Evaluate to what extent price is the most important element of the marketing mix for Tesco.

(12)

(Total for Question 7 = 25 marks)

TOTAL FOR SECTION C = 25 MARKS

TOTAL FOR PAPER = 90 MARKS

Answers

1. A gap in the market occurs when there is no business meeting the needs of customers for a particular good or service [1].
2. A [1]
3. **Any one of**: consumers are more health conscious [1], consumers are more environmentally aware [1], there is growing consumer demand for cafes and coffee shops [1].
4. The risks can be reduced by market research [1]. Entrepreneurial characteristics include risk taking [1]. There is a chance the business can be a success [1].
5. **Any three from**: consumers' needs can be met more closely [1], more choice [1], consumers can research different businesses and make a more informed decision before purchasing [1], competitive prices [1], convenience [1].
6. At the development stage [1].
7. Service is a non-physical product; an act carried out for you by someone else for money [1].
8. C [1]
9. A business needs to know what customers want in order to produce goods or services that meet customer needs [1]. Customers will purchase from the business [1], thereby increasing sales and profit [1]. **(1 mark for point made, with a further 2 marks available for explanation.)**
10. Added value is the difference between the cost of producing a good/service (raw materials/labour) and the price that consumers are willing to pay for it [1].
11. Success will depend on the type of business [1], the aims and objectives of the business [1], and the motives of the entrepreneur [1].
12. An owner invests their own money into a business [1]. If a small business is set up as a sole trader or partnership, there is unlimited liability, which means the owner's personal assets can be sold to pay the debts of the business [1].

1. So that the business can target a number of different customers [1]. This ensures that the business is current and on trend [1] and their customers do not go to competitors [1]. **(1 mark for point made, with a further 2 marks available for explanation.)**
2. To ensure that the business has enough customers [1] willing to pay a high enough price [1] to cover costs and make a profit [1]. **(1 mark for point made, with a further 2 marks available for explanation.)**
3. **Any three from**: more sales and revenue [1], leading to more profit [1], good customer reviews [1], repeat purchase/loyal customers [1].
4. The process of collecting information about what consumers want, market trends and competitors [1].
5. **Any two from**: to identify customer needs [1], find a gap in the market that is not being met [1], reduce the risks of running a business, to make better informed decisions [1].
6. Primary research can be expensive [1], time consuming [1] and results may be inaccurate [1].
7. The reliability of the data needs to be considered [1]; if market research is not collected in the correct way and from the right people [1], it can be misleading and unreliable [1]. **(1 mark for point made, with a further 2 marks available for explanation.)**
8. Quick and cheap [1]; Data is collected in real-time and so will be up-to-date [1]; Larger number of respondents [1].
9. Location [1]; Demographics [1]; Lifestyle [1]; Income [1]; Age [1].
10. **Any two from**: price [1], quality [1], range [1], colour [1].
11. Price [1]; Quality [1]; Location [1]; Product range [1]; Customer service [1].

12. Training staff in good customer service can increase training costs [1].

1. A cash-flow forecast shows when payments are due in and out of a business [1] to help a business plan ahead [1].
2. Cash surplus is when a business has more cash inflows than cash outflows [1]; then there is cash left over after paying bills [1].
3. a) February £12 000 – £13 000 = -£1000 [1], March £15 000 – £13 500 = £1500
   b) Opening balance: £14 000 [1], closing balance: £15 500 [1].
4. a)

	June (£)	July [£]
Receipts	27 400	25 800 [1]
Raw materials	7300	6900
Fixed costs	2600	2600 [1]
Total costs	9900	9500
Net cash-flow	17 500 [1]	16 300
Opening balance	21 300	38 800 [1]
Closing balance	38 800 [1]	55 100

   b) £6900 × 1.1 = £7590 raw materials [1] plus fixed costs of £2600 = £10 190 total costs [1]
   c) **Possible answer**: A cash-flow forecast can help predict cash inflows and outflows [1], which can help Daisy Chain establish whether there is enough cash to pay its bills on time [1] and allow time to raise finance if needed [1].
   Possible answer: A benefit would be to make a comparison between the actual inflows and outflows against the predicted inflows and outflows [1], which will help Daisy Chain highlight the areas where forecasts were inaccurate [1], in order to establish whether the forecast was incorrect, i.e. by being overoptimistic, or if there were unforseen financial circumstances [1].
   Possible answer: A cash-flow forecast can help predict cash inflows and outflows [1], which can help Daisy Chain establish whether there is a surplus of cash [1] that can be invested either in the business or in a savings account [1]. **(1 mark for benefit, with a further 2 marks available for explanation.)**
   d) Daisy Chain will need to ensure there is enough cash in the business to pay its bills on time [1] because if there is insufficient cash in the business, it faces risk of insolvency [1], which could cause the failure of the business [1].
   e) By receiving goods and selling them for cash before it has to pay its suppliers [1]. This would remove the need for Daisy Chain to raise its own capital for the purchase of goods [1] and help net cash-flow [1].
   f) Daisy Chain might not benefit from discounts [1].
   g) An overdraft facility can be arranged before any funds are needed [1] in case Daisy Chain spends all of its cash and needs to borrow from the bank on a short-term basis [1]. Daisy Chain will only pay interest for the amount and time borrowed [1].
   h) The interest rate is high [1] and the bank can stop the overdraft facility at any time [1].

1. A private limited company [1]. Rebecca will have limited liability so her personal savings are not at risk if the business is not successful [1]. She is able to sell shares to her friend [1]. Rebecca's friend can help to complete the accounts and paperwork required to submit to Companies House [1].

2. A business owned by one person [1]. Examples include: website designer/photographer/hairdresser [1]. **(Any suitable example will be accepted.)**
3. **Any two from:** Company accounts are available for the public to see [1], lots of administration to get started [1], shares cannot be sold to the public [1].
4. The place where a business operates [1].
5. Nature of the business [1]; Market [1]; Labour [1]; Materials [1]; Competitors [1].
6. Transport links need to be good so that supplies can be delivered easily and quickly [1] and finished products can be distributed [1].
7. Business can find out what customers want using online market research [1]. Businesses can then produce goods and services that meet these needs [1].
8. Modifying each element in the marketing mix allows a business to establish a differentiated good or service [1].
9. **Any one of:** Encourages customers to buy a business's products [1], creates awareness [1], boosts sales [1], builds a brand [1], communicates the features of a product [1].
10. **Any one of:** To borrow money from banks and lenders [1], attract potential investors [1], plan the business out [1], research legal responsibilities [1], reduce the risk of failure [1].
11. Aims and objectives are set out [1] and an entrepreneur can refer to these regularly [1] to ensure they are on track [1].
12. They will want to see forecast revenue, costs and profit [1] to determine if the business can pay back the money borrowed [1].
13. Some entrepreneurs will go with their gut instinct [1] and want to start a business straight away without spending any time putting a plan down on paper [1].

Pages 159–160 **Understanding External Influences on Business**

1. Groups of people who want to ensure businesses and governments act ethically [1] in relation to the environment/animal welfare/human rights [1].
2. **Possible answer:** The government wants businesses to do well so that more people are employed [1], leading to a reduction in unemployment levels [1], thereby reducing the amount of benefits the government has to pay out [1].
Possible answer: The government receives tax from businesses in the form of corporation tax [1], income tax from employees [1], and VAT from customers who have bought products from the business [1].
Possible answer: The government is a stakeholder in a business that is successful [1] because the business is producing more products/services [1], thereby contributing to a higher GDP [1]. **(1 mark for benefit, with a further 2 marks available for explanation.)**
3. The electronic ability [1] to transfer money quickly and safely from one bank account to another [1].
4. **Accept two from:** email [1], texts [1], websites [1], social media [1].
5. That workers have the right to work in a safe environment [1].
6. Goods or services shouldn't be faulty or damaged when the consumer receives them [1], and they should last a reasonable length of time [1].
7. The more people work, the more they earn and the more taxes they pay [1]. Also, if workers have money to spend, they demand more goods and services [1], which creates further selling opportunities for businesses [1].
8. In times of high unemployment it can be easier for businesses to recruit good quality staff because there are more unemployed workers looking for jobs [1], which means there are more applicants to choose from [1], allowing a business to recruit the most talented people [1].
9. The cost of borrowing [1] and the reward for saving [1].
10. The ASA tries to ensure that all advertising claims are accurate and true so consumers are not misled [1]. The ASA also deals with advertising complaints from consumers [1].
11. Consumers with borrowing tend to have to pay higher interest charges to banks [1], which means they have less disposable income [1], which results in customers spending less or buying inferior products [1].
12. Strong Pound, Imports Cheap, Exports Dear [1].

Pages 161–162 **Growing the Business**

1. The business can keep its values [1] because it has grown independently without having to compromise its beliefs [1], thereby protecting its brand identity [1].
2. When one large business buys a smaller business [1], which becomes part of the original bigger business [1].
3. It can take a while to sell the assets [1] and also the business may not receive the full cash value it is hoping for [1]. Also, it can look a bit desperate if a business wants to sell assets to raise cash [1].
4. **Any one of:** as a response to new innovation [1], new methods of working with technology [1], consumers using more technology [1], e-commerce selling methods [1], or similar response [1].
5. **Any one of:** seasonal work, e.g. Christmas or summer [1], sudden influx of demand from consumers in response to a successful advertising campaign [1], delayering the workforce if it gets too big [1], or similar response [1].
6. A business that produces and sells in more than one country [1].
7. A tax added onto the selling price of an imported good [1] to make it more expensive to buy in the UK [1].
8. Businesses and customers are able to buy and sell products anywhere in the world [1] now that it is easier to reach them due to digital communication [1].
9. When a consumer boycotts a product or a company the consumer is attempting to influence the behaviour of the company by not giving them any money [1].
10. A compromise between one thing and another [1]. **Possible example:** some businesses chose to use environmentally-friendly raw materials to attract customers but the trade-off is that the costs of the business are higher as a result. **(Any other reasonable example will be accepted.)**

Pages 163–164 **Making Marketing Decisions**

1. Cost [1]
2. Research, design and development costs are high [1] and sales are low as customers are unaware of the product [1]. A lot of money will be spent on promotion during this stage [1]. High costs and low sales mean the business will be making a loss [1].
3. Means a business may have to reduce their prices to remain competitive in the market [1].
4. Prices will be similar to competitors [1].
5. They will consider their market segment [1] and decide how best to reach that market segment [1].
6. **Any one of:** buy-one, get-one free [1], discount on the selling price [1], two-for-one [1].
7. They buy in large amounts from wholesalers or manufacturers [1] and make products available in local shops for customers [1].
8. Convenience [1], as customers can shop at any time from anywhere [1] and do not have to go to a physical shop [1]. **Other benefits:** more choice, delivery saves time for customers, accessibility as customers can shop at any time from anywhere. **(1 mark for benefit, with a further 2 marks available for explanation.)**
9. **Any one of:** dispatching orders quickly [1], various dispatch and delivery options [1], being available in locations and times convenient to customers can provide great customer satisfaction and repeat purchases and lead to possible competitive advantage [1].
10. The life cycle of the product may influence the promotion used for it [1]. Often when a product is new it will require lots of promotion [1], in contrast to the maturity stage when promotion takes place less [1]. **(1 mark for promotion, with a further 2 marks available for explanation.)**

11. The objectives of the business **[1]**; The market **[1]**; The size of a business **[1]**; The competition **[1]**; The nature of the product **[1]**.
12. Offer a price that is cheaper than competitors **[1]**.

Pages 165–166 **Making Operational Decisions**

1. One individual product is made at a time **[1]**. Once one product is made, another product can be started **[1]**.
2. **Any one of**: a breakdown in one of the lines **[1]**, impacts the entire production process **[1]**. Repetitive work **[1]** leads to low motivation for workers **[1]**. Not much flexibility **[1]**, so difficult to adapt production lines **[1]**. Machinery is expensive to buy **[1]** and assembly lines are expensive to set up **[1]**. **(1 mark for disadvantage, with a further 1 mark available for explanation.)**
3. Products are made in batches **[1]**, so raw materials or components can be purchased in large quantities, allowing the business to receive discounts, therefore the cost per unit is lower **[1]**.
4. Businesses do not hold any stock **[1]**. Raw materials and components are ordered in exactly when they are needed **[1]** and used straight away in the production process **[1]**.
5. A delay in the production process **[1]** and a business may not be able to meet demand **[1]**.
6. A business needs the best quality raw materials or services **[1]** for the best price **[1]**.
7. Quality control involves finished products being inspected to see if they meet minimum standards **[1]**. Quality assurance involves checking for quality during the production process **[1]**.
8. Quality will be high **[1]**, meaning less wastage from defective products **[1]**.
9. Customer expectations differ with different brands **[1]**. A business will need to research what their customers want **[1]** and match this to the quality standards that they set **[1]**. **(1 mark for point made, with a further 2 marks available for explanation.)**
10. By matching a customer's needs **[1]** to suitable products on offer by the business **[1]**.
11. Good relationships are built if customers receive a response to their feedback **[1]**. Positive and negative feedback is an effective source of market research for businesses **[1]**.
12. **Any one of**: happy customers **[1]**, more sales **[1]**, a positive working environment **[1]**, good reputation **[1]**, competitive advantage **[1]**.

Pages 167–168 **Making Financial Decisions**

1. Direct costs are costs that are directly linked with the production of the goods or service being produced and sold **[1]**.
2. Gross profit = sales revenue – cost of sales **[1]**
3. Net profit/loss = gross profit – other operating expenses and interest **[1]**
4. Revenue – total costs = profit **[1]**
   Therefore, revenue is 400 × £8 = £3200; Total costs are (400 × £1.80) + £930 = £1650 **[1]**.
   Therefore, net profit is £3200 – £1650 = £1550 **[1]**.
5. Profit is the amount of profit a business has made **[1]** whereas profitability looks at how good a business is at making a profit **[1]**.
6. The lower the gross profit margin, the more stock a business has to sell to make sustainable profit **[1]**.
7. ARR calculates how much an entrepreneur or investor is getting back on the money invested in a business **[1]** so they know how profitable their investment is **[1]**.
8. Average annual profit (total profit/no. of years)/cost of investment × 100 **[1]**
9. Financial data is the past, present and future records of the financial health of a business **[1]**.
10. **Any two from**: to show trends within a business **[1]**, banks will want to see financial data if they are considering a lending proposal **[1]**, investors will want to see financial data if they are considering investing in a business **[1]**.

Pages 169–170 **Making Human Resource Decisions**

1. Centralised organisation can slow communication between the shop-floor and senior management **[1]**.
2. **Any two from**: it can minimise mistakes **[1]**, speed up production **[1]**, improve service **[1]**.
3. When someone works the number of hours they are contracted to work but with more choice over when they work those hours **[1]**.
4. Employees who work with staff and have the authority to delegate work, and to reward and discipline staff **[1]**.
5. **Any two from**: notices in staff rooms **[1]**, emails **[1]**, management recommendation **[1]**, announcements at meetings **[1]**.
6. A CV is a summary of a person's career, education and skills **[1]**.
7. Application forms allow for specific questions to be asked **[1]** in a format that helps businesses treat all staff equally **[1]**.
8. **Any one of**: useful for teaching staff how to use specific equipment **[1]**, can be tailored to the employee in a familiar setting **[1]**, quick and cheap to arrange **[1]**.
9. **Any one of**: for staff to be able to carry out their roles effectively **[1]**, better quality goods and services **[1]**, more productivity **[1]**, higher levels of motivation **[1]**, to attract new recruits **[1]**, help staff retention **[1]**.
10. Once they have sold something **[1]**.
11. When staff are given short periods of time on various jobs before they move on to other jobs **[1]**.

Pages 171–185 **Exam Paper 1: Investigating small business**

The following marking guidance is relevant to **Question 3 (e)**, **Question 4 (b)** and **Question 5 (c)** in both Exam Paper 1 and Exam Paper 2.

Level	Mark	Descriptor
	0	No gradable material.
1	1–2	• Limited knowledge and understanding shown of relevant business concepts with limited terminology used. • Business information interpreted with limited development of points.
2	3–4	• Mostly correct knowledge and understanding of relevant business concepts shown, including appropriate terminology. • Business information interpreted with developed points but with some errors.
3	5–6	• Accurate knowledge and understanding of business concepts shown, including secure terminology used. • Business information interpreted with a chain of logical arguments.

The following marking guidance is relevant to **Question 6 (b)** and **Question 7 (c)** in Exam Paper 1.
The following marking guidance is relevant to **Question 6 (c)** and **Question 7 (d)** in Exam Paper 2.

Level	Mark	Descriptor
	0	No gradable material.
1	1–3	• Limited application of knowledge and understanding shown of relevant business concepts with limited terminology used. • Business information interpreted with limited development of points. • Simple judgement made with limited justification and with limited evaluation of the choices made.
2	4–6	• Mostly correct application of knowledge and understanding of relevant business concepts, including appropriate terminology.

		• Business information interpreted with developed points but with some errors. • A judgement is made with justification and relevant evaluation made.
3	7–9	• Accurate application of knowledge and understanding of business concepts shown, including secure terminology used. • Business information interpreted with a chain of logical arguments. • A thorough justification of the chosen judgement is made, based on detailed evaluation.

The following marking guidance is relevant to **Question 7 (d)** in Exam Paper 1 and **Question 7 (e)** in Exam Paper 2.

Level	Mark	Descriptor
	0	No gradable material.
1	1–4	• Limited knowledge and understanding of key terms shown with limited terminology used. • Limited application of knowledge and understanding of relevant business concepts, with limited terminology used. • Business information interpreted with limited development of points. • A simple judgement is made, with limited justification and limited evaluation of choices made.
2	5–8	• Mainly accurate knowledge and understanding with good use of terminology. • Mostly correct application of knowledge and understanding of relevant business concepts, including appropriate terminology. • Business information interpreted with developed points but with some errors. • A judgement made with justification and relevant evaluation.
3	9–12	• Sound knowledge and understanding shown, with accurate terminology used throughout. • Accurate application of knowledge and understanding of business concepts, including secure terminology used. • Business information interpreted with a chain of logical arguments. • A thorough justification of chosen judgement and detailed evaluation made.

Pages 172–177: SECTION A

1. (a) A [1]
   (b) C [1]
   (c) **Possible answer**: A business can benefit from effective customer service because it is likely to generate increased revenue from repeat purchases [1]. As customers enjoy their experience of the business it will encourage them to buy the same products again [1], thus increasing the revenue of the business [1].
   Possible answer: A business will have an improved brand image [1], as customers will enjoy the products they have purchased and increase their perception of the quality of the products offered [1]. They can also use social media to share with other customers their positive experiences, which will improve the business's brand image [1]. **(1 mark for identifying a benefit, with a further 2 marks available for explaining the benefit. Any responses that list more than one benefit with no/limited explanation will gain a maximum of 1 mark.)**

(d) **Possible answer**: Limited liability decreases the personal risk of the owners [1] for a private limited company. This is due to the fact that the owners are not personally responsible for the debt owed by the business [1]. Thus, the owners can only lose the money invested into the business [1].
Possible answer: The owners are not responsible for the debts of the business [1]. They have a separate legal identity [1] so this means that there is less personal risk to the owners [1]. **(1 mark for identifying an advantage, with a further 2 marks available for explanation. Any responses that list more than one advantage with no/limited explanation will gain a maximum of 1 mark.)**

2. (a) A [1]
   (b) A [1]; D [1]
   (c)

	November (£)	December (£)
Total receipts	18 400	20 200 [1]
Stock	7050	10 000
Fixed costs	3200	3200
Total payments	10 250	13 200 [1]
Net cash-flow	8150 [1]	7000
Opening balance	5400	13 550
Closing balance	13 550 [1]	20 550 [1]

(1 mark for each correct figure. Full marks will be awarded for the correct responses even if there is no evidence of workings.)

(d) **Possible answer**: A business could add value to the chocolate bar by changing the taste [1]. They could do this by adding new ingredients, which can improve the quality of the product [1]. If the quality of the product is higher, customers are willing to pay more for the product [1].
Possible answer: A business could create a unique selling point by using celebrities to advertise the product [1]. This will make the product more distinctive [1], making customers willing to pay more for the product [1]. **(1 mark for identifying a method, with a further 2 marks available for explaining the method. Any responses that list more than one method with no/limited explanation will gain a maximum of 1 mark.)**

   (e) A [1]
3. (a) D [1]
   (b) Variable cost = £1.50 × 500 = £750 [1]
   Total cost = fixed cost + variable cost
   £2000 + £750 = £2750 [1] **(The full 2 marks will be awarded for the correct response even if there is no evidence of workings.)**

(c) **Possible answer**: A conflict that can exist between the customer and the shareholder is the price of the products [1]. Customers want the best value for money so want the price to be as low as possible [1]. However, if the prices are very low shareholders are likely to make less profit due to a decrease in revenue [1].
Possible answer: A conflict can exist as the customers want the best quality products so they enjoy their purchase [1]. However, this will be expensive as the firm will have to pay for research and development or more expensive materials [1]. This is likely to decrease the profit of the business due to increased costs [1]. **(1 mark for identifying a suitable conflict, with a further 2 marks available for explanation.**

Any responses that list a conflict with no/limited explanation will gain a maximum of 1 mark.)

(d) **Possible answer**: Customers can benefit from an increased range of products available **[1]**. As there are many competitors, customers will have greater access to products **[1]**. This means they have more options to choose the best quality product or one that best suits their needs **[1]**.

Possible answer: Customers can benefit from cheaper prices **[1]**. As many businesses are competing to make sales they are likely to reduce their prices to attract price-sensitive customers **[1]**. Thus customers are much more likely to get better value for money for the products they require **[1]**. **(1 mark for identifying an advantage, with a further 2 marks available for explaining the advantage chosen. Any responses that list one advantage with no/limited explanation will gain a maximum of 1 mark.)**

(e) The following content is indicative of what the answer requires.
- Price sensitivity of the customers.
- The level of competition.
- If their customers are not price-sensitive then the business will be able to charge a higher price for their products without having a significant impact on sales volume.
- This might impact the price charged as more competition will force a business to charge lower prices to remain competitive.

(6 marks are available for this question; see marking table on page 201 for guidance.)

Pages 178–182: SECTION B

4. (a) **Possible answer**: By using a survey **[1]** Peter will be able to easily analyse trends in the needs of his customers using statistics gained from this research method. This will allow him to gain opinions on a large scale **[1]**.

Possible answer: Through using an interview **[1]** Peter will be able to identify detailed opinions of his customers to see why they may not be happy with the queuing times **[1]**. **(2 marks for a developed point outlining an appropriate primary research method; a maximum of 1 mark will be awarded if the point is not developed.)**

(b) The following content is indicative of what the answer requires.
- Ordering online means fewer customers need to travel to the store, which will mean the queuing times will be shorter.
- As queuing times are shorter, this is likely to enhance the experience of the customer, which improves the brand image, as the store/cards are more likely to get positive customer reviews.
- As customer needs have been improved, this is likely to generate repeat purchases as customers have enjoyed their experience and are likely to buy cards again from the business.
- The better the brand image, the more likely Harris's Celebrations is to gain new customers due to customers hearing positive reviews of the business.

(6 marks are available for this question; see marking table on page 201 for guidance.)

5. (a) **Possible answer**: By having high-quality cards Peter has a unique selling point over his competitors **[1]**. This is likely to result in a positive brand image as customers will see Peter's cards as being better than his competitors' cards **[1]**.

Possible answer: Having high-quality cards can give Peter a competitive advantage **[1]**. This is likely to result in repeat purchases as customers are more likely to purchase Peter's cards as they are better quality **[1]**. **(2 marks will be awarded for a developed point outlining a benefit; a maximum of 1 mark will be awarded if the point is not developed.)**

(b) £225 × 24 = £5400 **[1]**
£5400 – £5000 = £400 **[1]**
(You are strongly recommended to show your working.)

(c) The following content is indicative of what the answer requires.
- A loan would be able to provide the substantial amount of money needed by Peter. Unlike other sources of finance, Peter would not lose any control or ownership of his business by taking out a loan.
- In the long term a bank loan will cost Peter more than he borrowed in the first place. This means that the fixed costs will increase. Some of Peter's customers may prefer to buy the products in Peter's store, so the business has increased costs without increasing revenue.
- The bank may want to put security on the loan, which means a greater risk for Peter in case he is unable to pay them back – he would lose his assets or personal possessions.
- As the fixed costs have increased due to loan repayments, it means that Peter may have to charge higher prices in the long term. This may deter price-sensitive customers from purchasing Peter's products.

(6 marks are available for this question; see marking table on page 201 for guidance.)

6. (a) Break-even point = fixed cost/contribution per unit **[1]**
£10 000/(£3 – £1) **[1]** = 5000 units **[1]** **(Full marks will be awarded for the correct response even if there is no evidence of workings.)**

(b) The following content is indicative of what the answer requires.
- Increased advertisement will increase customer awareness of the business.
- Reduced prices might increase revenue as price-sensitive customers are more likely to buy the cards.
- This is important as Peter's business is new and he will need to make customers aware of his products in order to increase the shop's customer base.
- As Peter's business is new, lower prices may encourage customers to buy the products for the first time.
- Increasing advertising would be a more appropriate option as the more customers are aware of the business, the quicker Peter can increase his revenue from a bigger customer base.
- Lower prices would be a more appropriate option as customers are more likely to buy the products for the first time if the prices are cheaper, which is more likely to increase revenue than advertising.

(9 marks are available for this question; see marking table on pages 201–202 for guidance.)

Pages 183–185: SECTION C

7. (a) **Any one of**: product **[1]**, place **[1]**, price **[1]**, promotion **[1]**.

(b) Variable costs, **any one of**: milk, sugar **[1]**, vegetable oil **[1]**, salt **[1]**, cocoa butter **[1]**, almonds **[1]**. Then, **any two from**: the total cost of sugar is going to increase with output **[1]**. The more products demanded in the ice-cream shop, the more sugar the business will need to purchase **[1]**. This will cause the variable cost to rise **[1]**.

(c) The following content is indicative of what the answer requires.
- If Courtney starts off as a sole trader, he will be able to make all of his own decisions.
- If Courtney starts off as a private limited company, he will have less personal risk due to having limited liability.
- He has experience in the industry as a store manager so he should be able to make his own decisions without having to consult others. This in turn means that he gets to keep all the profits that his business will make due to being the sole owner of the business. In a private limited company it is likely that he would have to share the profits amongst the shareholders.
- If the business fails, Courtney will be personally responsible for all the debts of the business. Ice-cream is a luxury item and is likely to be something customers sacrifice during a downturn in the economy. There are also three already established ice-cream shops, which means that there is a risk that Courtney's business may fail and result in personal financial risk.
- On balance, opening as a sole trader would be a better option as Courtney has experience and would therefore be able to make his own decisions, resulting in keeping all

the business profit, which would have to be shared in a private limited company.
- Opening as a private limited company would be a better option as Courtney is competing in a market that already has established competitors and is a high risk with regard to downturns in the economy. This means that by having limited liability he will have less personal risk as a private limited company.

(9 marks are available for this question; see marking table on pages 201–202 for guidance.)

Helpful Tips
Make sure you have a clear final judgement at the end of a response that is based on the arguments you have made. Never make a judgement at the beginning of your answer, as you must argue first before making a decision.

(d) The following content is indicative of what the answer requires.
- Courtney has shown himself to be innovative, which is an important entrepreneurial skill for a business to succeed in a competitive market.
- A small business selling ice-cream is likely to suffer if there is a downturn in the economy.
- Courtney has experience of making and selling ice-cream and has conducted market research, gaining a good knowledge of the market. He identified a gap in the market, which current competitors are not filling.
- If there is a downturn, customers are less likely to spend money and in particular on luxury products such as ice-cream.
- Identifying a gap in the market for low-calorie ice-cream creates a unique selling point, which is likely to attract customer demand for this specific type of product.
- In a recession a luxury good such as ice-cream is likely to be sacrificed in spending, resulting in less revenue for Courtney's business.
- Despite having established competition in the market, Courtney has a unique selling point, which is likely to allow the business to succeed, as the target market has clearly identified this as a need to be filled.
- On balance, Courtney's business carries too great a risk as a downturn in the economy will significantly reduce the demand for ice-cream products. Also, there is already competition, meaning Courtney's business will have to try and persuade customers from existing businesses to trial their products.

(12 marks are available for this question; see marking table on page 202 for guidance.)

Pages 186–198 Exam Paper 2: Building a business

Pages 187–191: SECTION A

1. (a) A [1]
   (b) A [1]
   (c) **Possible answer**: A business can benefit from having a unique selling point [1] where customers see the product as distinct from the competition [1]. This is likely to generate sales as customers are better able to recognise the product [1]. **Possible answer**: A business can benefit from having a competitive advantage [1], as it is able to offer a product that is higher quality [1] than the competition. This is likely to result in a higher number of sales as customers will prefer the business's product to the competition's product [1]. **(1 mark for identifying a benefit, with 2 further marks available for explaining the benefit. Any responses that list more than one benefit with no/limited explanation will gain a maximum of 1 mark.)**

Helpful Tips
A lot of these types of questions are looking at how a business differentiates from their competitors. Use business terms such as 'unique selling point' and 'competitive advantage' – then refer to how these are likely to encourage increased revenue.

(d) **Possible answer**: An advantage of on-the-job training is that it is more cost effective than any other form of training [1]. This is because existing staff generally train new staff while they are working so the company does not have to pay to train staff externally [1]. This means that costs are lower, which means lower fixed costs [1]. **Possible answer**: An advantage of on-the-job training is that it is more productive [1]. If workers are learning while they are working, they are fulfilling roles in the business that would not be filled if they were learning off site [1]. This shows that a business is able to produce more if workers are learning on the job [1]. **(1 mark for identifying an advantage, with 2 marks available for explaining the advantage. Any responses that list more than one advantage with no/limited explanation will gain a maximum of 1 mark.)**

2. (a) D [1]; E [1]
   (b) A [1]; C [1]
   (c) Net profit margin = net profit/sales × 100 [1] £55 000/£220 000 × 100 = 25% [1] **(You will be awarded full marks for the correct response even if there is no evidence of workings.)**

Helpful Tips
Have a clear understanding that net profit is gross profit minus total overheads. The percentage should always be less than the gross profit margin.

(d) **Possible answer**: A barrier to communication is when it is excessive [1]. If an employee receives too much information, it is likely to be forgotten or lost [1]. This means that they may not be able to perform the task to the best of their ability, as they have not gained the information required to complete the task [1]. **Possible answer**: A barrier to communication can be that information may not be interpreted correctly [1]. If an employee is given information verbally, the information may be forgotten [1], which can result in a task being completed incorrectly [1]. **(1 mark for identifying a barrier, with 2 marks available for explaining the barrier. Any responses that list more than one barrier with no/limited explanation will gain a maximum of 1 mark.)**
(e) **Possible answer**: Having higher levels of buffer stock means more storage space is required [1]. If the stock is perishable, it means that it is more likely to be wasted [1]. This means increased costs but no increased revenue for the business [1]. **(1 mark for identifying a suitable disadvantage, with 2 marks available for explaining the disadvantage. Any responses that list more than one disadvantage with no/limited explanation will gain a maximum of 1 mark.)**

Helpful Tips
Always consider the types of stock that a business might hold. Stock that is technological can become obsolete very quickly so it is important that a business does not hold too much stock of this type or they will be unable to sell it in the future.

3. (a) B [1]
   (b) Total revenue = selling price × quantity [1] £50 × (200 + 300) = £25 000 [1]

(c) **Possible answer**: It is likely to increase worker motivation as they will be financially rewarded for good performance [1]. This means that the business is likely to retain its workers as they are more motivated [1]. This in turn will increase the revenue for the business through increased sales [1].
Possible answer: As workers are being paid based on how many sales they produce [1] they are likely to work a lot harder. This is likely to result in higher sales as the workers are more effective in their job [1]. This means greater revenue for the business [1]. **(1 mark for identifying a suitable reason for paying commission, with 2 marks available for explaining the reason chosen. Any responses that list one reason with no/limited explanation will gain a maximum of 1 mark.)**

(d) **Possible answer**: If the workers are motivated then they are likely to be more productive [1]. This results in cheaper unit costs for the business [1]. This means that the business can charge more competitive prices [1].
Possible answer: If the workers are motivated, they are less likely to leave the business [1]. This reduces the costs associated with trying to recruit a new worker and train them [1]. This means that the business can charge more competitive prices [1]. **(1 mark for identifying a benefit, with 2 marks available for explaining the benefit chosen. Any responses that list one benefit with no/limited explanation will gain a maximum of 1 mark.)**

(e) The following content is indicative of what the answer requires.
- Clear roles and responsibilities for each worker.
- Chances of being promoted up the organisation.
- This means employees are more productive as they know who they report to and what their responsibilities are.
- An employee has clear routes for promotion at work so they can move up the structure. This is likely to increase motivation – employees work harder in order to develop their career.
(6 marks are available for this question; see marking table on page 201 for guidance.)

Pages 192–195: SECTION B

4. (a) **Possible answer**: The use of social media allows the business to create a greater awareness of the brand to its target market [1]. As the business is able to reach a much wider range of customers it allows it to promote its products, leading to an increase in revenue [1].
Possible answer: The use of social media is a much cheaper form of promotion over traditional methods such as advertisement [1]. The cheaper method of promotion allows variable costs to be lowered, which allows the business to charge more competitive prices [1]. **(2 marks will be awarded for a developed point outlining the impact of social media on the promotion of products. A maximum of 1 mark will be awarded if the point is not developed.)**

(b) The following content is indicative of what the answer requires.
- If Shaketastic charges a higher price for its products, it is able to break even more quickly.
- If Shaketastic charges a higher price, it may lose customers if they are price-sensitive.
- This means that Shaketastic does not have to achieve the same sales volume in order to break even. If customers are not price-sensitive, then revenue is likely to increase for the business.
- Customers may no longer see the products as value for money and may turn to rival businesses that offer more competitive prices.
(6 marks are available for this question; see marking table on page 201 for guidance.)

Helpful Tips
Always relate your responses to the case study, as this should influence the judgement you make for this question. Are they established? Do they have a strong brand image? If the business has a strong brand image, customers are more willing to pay a higher price.

5. (a) The use of brand names allows customers to instantly recognise businesses they have previously purchased from [1]. This means that they are much more likely to trial the product due to previous positive experiences with these particular brands, e.g. Nutella [1]. **(2 marks will be awarded for a developed point outlining an appropriate benefit. Only 1 mark will be awarded if the point is not developed.)**

(b) **Possible answer**: A limitation of higher buffer stock is that the ingredients they purchase are perishable [1]. If the stock is not demanded then the stock will be wasted as food will expire and not be used [1].
Possible answer: A limitation of higher buffer stock is that more storage space is required [1]. Shaketastic may not have the resources in their stores to hold the stock, particularly as some stock may need to be refrigerated [1]. **(2 marks will be awarded for a developed point outlining an appropriate limitation. Only 1 mark will be awarded if the point is not developed.)**

(c) The following content is indicative of what the answer requires.
- Job production may be a preferred method as customers may require customised milkshakes.
- Batch production may be a preferred method for the more popular products as they can be made more quickly, which would reduce queuing times for customers.
- Job production would allow Shaketastic to tailor-make some of the products in order to meet the needs of the customer. The higher the customer satisfaction, the more likely they are to repeat purchase.
- If the queuing times are reduced, customers are more likely to enjoy their experience at Shaketastic. This is likely to result in repeat purchases.
(6 marks are available for this question; see marking table on page 201 for guidance.)

Helpful Tips
For these types of questions there is no one correct answer – only justification. For any point you make you must justify why this would be an appropriate method specifically for the business.

6. (a) Total cost = fixed cost + variable cost [1]
(b) As the products are milkshakes/smoothies, they need to be kept at a low temperature [1]. This means that Shaketastic need a vehicle that can store these products at this temperature, which can be expensive [1]. **(2 marks will be awarded for a developed point outlining an appropriate limitation. Only 1 mark will be awarded if the point is not developed.)**

(c) The following content is indicative of what the answer requires.
- Through offering a wider product range it can create a competitive advantage for the business.
- Ordering cheaper materials would reduce the costs of the business.
- If the customers like the new flavours Shaketastic creates, this would create a unique selling point over rival competitors, attracting more customers to purchase products from Shaketastic.

- This results in lower costs and means the business could charge more competitive prices than its rivals, which will generate more revenue.
- Offering a wider product range is a more appropriate option as it will create a competitive advantage for Shaketastic over their rivals and encourage customers to purchase from the business.
- Ordering cheaper raw materials is a more appropriate option as it will reduce the costs for the business, which means more competitive prices can be offered to give customers greater value for money. The greater the value for money, the more likely it is that customers will repeat purchase, increasing Shaketastic's profit.
(9 marks are available for this question; see marking table on pages 201–202 for guidance.)

Helpful Tips
You will gain much higher marks if you make fewer points but have more detailed analysis of the points you do make. The more critical you are, the higher the marks. If appropriate, counter-argue your points.

Pages 196–198: SECTION C
7. **(a)** **Any one of**: demographic [1], lifestyle [1], income [1], age [1], location [1].
   (b) A customer is a person that purchases a good or service [1].
   (c) An increase in the quality of Tesco's products means that customers will see Tesco's products as better value for money [1], which will make Tesco more competitive against its rivals Lidl and Aldi [1]. **(2 marks for a developed point outlining a benefit. Only 1 mark will be awarded if the point is not developed.)**
   (d) The following content is indicative of what the answer requires.
   - If Tesco employs fewer staff, its labour costs will decrease.
   - If Tesco outsources its product to cheaper manufacturers, its cost of production will decrease.
   - As customers have left Tesco to go to cheaper competitors Aldi and Lidl, if Tesco has lower costs then it is able to offer cheaper prices. This reduces the advantages of Tesco's rivals and encourages those price-sensitive customers who left Tesco to return to Tesco. However, if Tesco has too few staff then its store service might slip as staff might not be able to cope with demand.
   - As Tesco struggles to compete on price, then having lower costs means it is able to offer cheaper prices

to compete with Aldi and Lidl. However, purchasing products from abroad can take longer to transport and these products are at more risk of delivery delays, which can impact on store service.
   - On balance, reducing staff is a better option as long as Tesco has enough workers to operate its stores. It would mean that if Tesco was able to meet demand, its labour costs will be lower, meaning it is able to offer cheaper prices to be more competitive against discounter rivals.
   - On balance, outsourcing manufacturing abroad will reduce costs, which means that Tesco can still offer the same service as its staff levels are the same but it can also offer cheaper costs via cheap imports. This means Tesco is able to compete with price discounters Aldi and Lidl.
   (9 marks are available for this question; see marking table on pages 201–202 for guidance.)
   (e) The following content is indicative of what the answer requires.
   - Price is the only element of the marketing mix that will generate revenue for Tesco.
   - Product may be a more important factor as price is often a reflection of the quality of the products purchased.
   - Tesco clearly has been losing sales due to price, as Tesco initially raised its prices, resulting in customers turning to discounters Lidl and Aldi.
   - If Tesco has higher quality products, such as their Tesco Finest range, customers would be willing to pay more money.
   - Therefore, price has a significant impact on customers, particularly as grocery shopping is a large household expenditure. As Tesco has raised its prices it has made record losses, showing a link between price and profit margins.
   - If customers purchase a poor quality product then they will probably not have a positive experience, which is less likely to result in repeat purchase.
   - Therefore price is the most important element of the marketing mix for Tesco due to the high level of price competition from discounters Lidl and Aldi.
   - On balance, product is a more important element of the marketing mix as customers are unlikely to repeat purchase products that do not meet their customer needs. The higher the quality of products, the more customers are willing to pay for the products.
   (12 marks are available for this question; see marking table on page 202 for guidance.)

Notes

ACKNOWLEDGEMENTS

The author and publisher are grateful to the copyright
holders for permission to use quoted materials and images.

All images © Shutterstock.com

Every effort has been made to trace copyright holders and obtain their
permission for the use of copyright material. The author and publisher will
gladly receive information enabling them to rectify any error or omission in
subsequent editions. All facts are correct at time of going to press.

Published by Collins
An imprint of HarperCollins*Publishers* Ltd
1 London Bridge Street
London SE1 9GF

HarperCollins*Publishers*
1st Floor, Watermarque Building
Ringsend Road, Dublin 4, Ireland

© HarperCollins*Publishers* Limited 2020

ISBN 9780008227395

First published 2017
This edition published 2020

10 9 8 7 6

British Library Cataloguing in Publication Data.

A CIP record of this book is available from the British Library.

Authored by: Stephanie Campbell, Helen Kellaway and Tony Michaelides
Commissioning Editors: Katherine Wilkinson and Charlotte Christensen
Editor: Charlotte Christensen
Project Manager: Jill Laidlaw
Cover Design: Kevin Robbins and Sarah Duxbury
Inside Concept Design: Sarah Duxbury and Paul Oates
Text Design and Layout: Jouve India Private Limited
Production: Natalia Rebow
Printed and Bound in the UK using 100% Renewable
Electricity at CPI Group (UK) Ltd

MIX
Paper from
responsible source
FSC www.fsc.org   FSC™ C007454

This book is produced from independently
certified FSC™ paper to ensure responsible
forest management.

For more information visit:
www.harpercollins.co.uk/green